Family Handbook

of

Christian Knowledge

THE BIBLE

Family Handbook

of

Christian Knowledge

THE BIBLE

Editor
JOSH McDOWELL

Written by

DON STEWART

CAMPUS CRUSADE FOR CHRIST

Published by

HERE'S LIFE PUBLISHERS, INC.

San Bernardino, California 92402

Family Handbook of Christian Knowledge: THE BIBLE
Josh McDowell, Editor
Written by Don Stewart

A Campus Crusade for Christ Book
Published by
HERE'S LIFE PUBLISHERS, INC.
P.O. Box 1576
San Bernardino, CA 92402

ISBN 0-86605-103-1
Library of Congress Catalogue Card 83-070194
HLP Product No. 403089
©Copyright 1983 by Campus Crusade for Christ, Inc.

Adapted from the book originally written by
Willem J.J. Glashouwer and Willem J. Ouweneel,
and published in Dutch under the title:
    "Het ontstaan van de Bijbel"
    Published by: Stichting "De Evangelische Omroep"
        Oude Amersfoortseweg 79a
        1200 AN HILVERSUM
        The Netherlands
    Originally published in 1979.
Unless otherwise indicated, Scripture quotations are from the New American
Standard Bible, ©The Lockman Foundation 1960, 1962, 1963, 1968, 1971, 1972,
1973, 1975, and are used by permission.

TABLE OF CONTENTS

INTRODUCTION

Abraham Lincoln once said, "The Bible is the best gift God has ever given to man. All the good from the Savior of the world is communicated to us through this book."

The Bible is the greatest book ever written. It contains the answers to the most important questions of life: "Who am I?" "Why am I here?" "Where am I going?" "What is life all about?" The Bible has been called the Book of Life since it gives significance to all people's lives. It proclaims that Jesus Christ is Lord, the ruler and Savior of all creation. Let us look at this "Book of Books," examining its composition, its survival over the centuries and its inspiration. Together we will see some of the things that make the Bible the Life-giving Holy Scripture it is.

CHAPTER ONE

The Bible—Not Just Another Book

The caves of Qumran, near the Dead Sea, where in 1947 the Dead Sea Scrolls were discovered.

When printing was invented the Bible was often the first book in a given language that came off the press. This Dutch Bible is an example of the primitive art of printing.

The present volume will discuss the making of the Old and New Testaments, how the "canon" of Scripture was compiled, the contents of the apocryphal books, the inspiration of Scripture, the historical reliability of the Old and New Testaments and the contents of the Old and New Testaments.

The Bible stands above all other books in the world. In this chapter we will discuss ten factors that contribute to its uniqueness as God's Holy Word.

What objective evidence do we have in support of the inspiration and reliability of the Bible? Chapter two discusses the trustworthiness of the Old Testament text. Has the text of the Old Testament remained accurate throughout history? Does it read the same today as when it was written? Can we trust that the words we have are an accurate representation of the original?

Chapter three will present the same kind of case for the text of the New Testament. Have its words been preserved correctly? From chapters two and three we can conclude that our present English Bible is a trustworthy representation of the original.

Once we have determined that, we will look at the Bible's contents, the Biblical canon, i.e., those books accepted as the Christian Scriptures. In chapter four we will show why the specific books we find in our Bible today deserve the designation "Holy Scripture," and why certain other traditionally revered books are not of the caliber of the canonical books.

Chapter five is a comprehensive review of Biblical inspiration. What do we mean when we say that the Bible is inspired? Why are these books on a different level from other literature? When we say "inspired," what exactly do we mean? Is the Bible inspired in the sense that it touches its readers emotionally, like fine poetry? Is it inspired in the sense that some of what it says is in accord with what God says? Or is it inspired in the sense that it is God's specific, inerrant revelation to humankind?

Chapter six will deal with the historical reliability of the Old Testament. We need to see through additional evidence that what was accurately transmitted over the centuries is also historically trustworthy. We will look at some of the archaeological and historical evidence available to confirm the trustworthiness of the Old Testament.

Chapter seven will do the same for the New Testament. We will see through representative examples that we can trust the historical reliability of the New Testament documents.

This volume will conclude with two chapters describing the contents of the Holy Scriptures. We will discuss the story of God and His people as revealed in the pages of the Old Testament. We will see God's plan for His people unfolding through the ages. In our review of New Testament contents we will note the exciting events of the incarnation — when Jesus Christ, the Son of God, became a human being to bring us salvation. We will see the dynamic growth of the early church, as the disciples of Jesus Christ proclaimed salvation in the name of their risen Lord throughout the known world. We will see the contents of the Bible transforming lives.

When the Dutch Bible was printed in 1477 it contained only the Old Testament, yet it was so large it was bound in two volumes.

It is our desire that this book will inspire readers' interest in reading and studying the Bible itself. There are thousands of books *about* the Bible: there is only one Word of God.

The Wonders of the Bible

Most of us have heard of the "wonders of the world," including the pyramids of Egypt, the hanging gardens of ancient Babylon, the Colossus at Rhodes, and so on. There are also "wonders" of the Bible, characteristics that set the Bible apart from all other literature, ancient and modern. Let's look at ten of these "wonders of the Bible."

The Wonder of Its Unity

One of the amazing characteristics of the Bible is its unity. That unity is evident in spite of its being a compilation of books done over a long period of time. The Bible is composed of 66 separate books, 39 in the Old Testament and 27 in the New Testament. Yet those 66 books form a cohesive whole, one dynamic message of God's dealings with humankind.

The 66 books of the Bible were composed over a period of around 1,500 years. The first books written probably were what we know as the books of Moses or the Law of Moses (Genesis, Exodus, Leviticus, Numbers and

The Old Testament was originally composed in two languages, Hebrew and Aramaic. The section on top is in Hebrew and comes from the Leningrad Codex, written about A.D. 1000. Below is an Aramaic fragment dating two centuries before Christ.

Deuteronomy), composed around 1400 B.C. This assumes an archaeological dating of 1445 B.C. for the Exodus. Others cite 1290 B.C. [This chronology is dealt with further in the third book of this series.] The book of Job might have been written earlier, but we have little evidence to tie it to a specific period before the books of Moses. The last of the New Testament was written around A.D. 90, and includes the writings of the apostle John (the Gospel of John, 1, 2, and 3 John, and Revelation). Genesis through Revelation involves a time span of around 1,500 years.

These 66 books were composed by over 40 authors, from a variety of educational and cultural backgrounds. Joshua, for example, (who wrote the end of Deuteronomy and the book of Joshua) was a military general; Daniel the prophet was a prime minister; Amos was a shepherd, Luke a physician, Paul a rabbi, Peter and John fishermen, and Nehemiah a court servant. Thus, the writers' backgrounds were remarkably diverse.

The books of the Bible were composed in a variety of places and cultures. Ezekiel wrote his work while a captive in Babylon. The apostle Paul wrote some of his letters from prison in Rome. David the king wrote some of his psalms while he was a fugitive in the wilderness. Jeremiah wrote while he was in a dungeon. The books were written on three continents: Africa, Asia, and Europe.

13

The Bible was composed in three languages. The Old Testament was written mostly in Hebrew, with a small part in Aramaic. The New Testament was composed in the common Greek of the day, *Koine*.

The Bible deals consistently with a variety of controversial subjects such as the origin of the universe, the existence and nature of God, the nature and purpose of humankind, and the origin and extent of evil.

One would expect that the result of such diversity would be a hodge-podge of contradictory literature, a chaotic text, full of contradictions and distortions. We see the wonder of the Bible in that it is completely consistent, coherent and trustworthy. None of the authors or books is either internally, of themselves, or externally contradictory. The Bible's remarkable unity, its continually unfolding story of redemption, is a true wonder.

The unity of the teachings of the Bible is consistent from beginning to end. These teachings include the following:

man — his origin, his fall, his redemption, his earthly and eternal destiny

sin — its beginning, its consequences, its punishment in this world and the next

Satan — the instigator of evil, the liar and murderer from the beginning, his war against God and against believers, his final judgment

Israel — her social and political development, idolatry, preservation and final destiny

the church — her history, from her establishment to her glorification

salvation — its provision, according to the divine plan, as we have outlined it in the paragraph above

repentance, faith, the life of the believer, prayer, the service of God, etc. — subjects for infinitely rewarding study, carrying us through the entire Bible

the Holy Spirit — present at creation, pronouncing the last prayer of the Bible (Gen. 1:2; Rev. 22:17)

God — forever the same, in His sovereignty, His eternality, His spirituality, His omnipotence, His uniqueness, His omniscience,

His omnipresence, His holiness, His righteousness and His love
Jesus Christ — the theme par excellence of all the written revelation.[1]

Some time ago, in another book, we issued a challenge concerning this wonder of the Bible. That challenge is repeated here, in the confidence that it still stands:

"Lest anyone think this [unity] isn't something marvelous, we'd like to give you this challenge. Find ten people from your local area who have similar educational backgrounds — all speak the same language, and all are from basically the same culture — then separate them and ask them to write their opinion on only one controversial subject, such as the meaning of life.

"When they have finished, compare the conclusions of these ten writers. Do they agree with each other? Of course not. But the Bible did not consist of merely ten authors, but 40. It was not written in one generation, but over a period of 1,500 years; not by authors with the same education, culture and language, but with vastly different education, many different cultures, from three continents and three different languages, and finally not just one subject but hundreds.

"And yet the Bible is a unity. There is complete harmony, which cannot be explained by coincidence or collusion. The unity of the Bible is a strong argument in favor of its divine inspiration.

"The unity of the Scriptures is only one reason among many which support the Bible's claim to be the divine Word of God. Others which could be explained in detail are the testimony of the early Church, the witness of history and archaeology, and the evidence of changed lives throughout the centuries, to name but a few.

"These factors led the great archaeologist, W. F. Albright, to conclude, 'The Bible towers in content above all earlier religious literature; and it towers just as impressively over all subsequent literature in the direct simplicity of its message and the catholicity of its appeal to men of all lands and times' *(The Christian Century,* November, 1958).

"The Bible is special. It is unique. No other book has any such credentials. No other book even comes close. 'England has two books, the Bible and Shakespeare. England made Shakespeare, but the Bible made England' (Victor Hugo, cited by Mead, *Encyclopedia of Religious Quotations,* p. 49)."[2]

The Wonder of Its Historical Accuracy

Another feature that separates the Bible from other ancient literature is its meticulous fidelity to historical accuracy. Within the pages of the Bible we find countless references to events, people and places. The science of archaeology along with secular historical records confirm the precision of the references in the various biblical books. The minute attention to detail observed by the biblical writers is unparalleled in any other ancient literature. Nelson Glueck, a famous Jewish archaeologist, observed, "It may be stated categorically that no archaeological discovery has ever controverted a biblical reference.... [I assert] the almost incredibly accurate historical memory of the Bible, and particularly so when it is fortified by archaeological fact"[3]

Because the historical evidence in support of the Bible is so great, chapters six and seven are devoted to exploring some of that evidence. But even from this short overview, we can see that the Bible's historical accuracy is truly a wonder.

The Wonder of Its Indestructibility

The fact that the complete text of the Bible has survived throughout history is a wonderful testimony to the preserving power of God. The Scriptures have survived time, persecution, and criticism.

The first book of the Bible was composed some 3,500 years ago; the last was completed nearly 2,000 years ago. The original manuscripts were all written on perishable surfaces and have long since disappeared. The thousands of copies we possess, however, accurately represent the originals.

A section from the Isaiah Scroll found in the caves of Qumran. This scroll dates back one hundred years before the birth of Christ.

Through the science of textual criticism, from those copies we can arrive at a very close reproduction of the originals. The overwhelming manuscript evidence of the text of the Old and New Testaments affirms that the text of the Bible has not only survived throughout the centuries, but has survived virtually unchanged. We will develop this point further in our chapters on the reliability of the Old and New Testaments.

The Bible has also survived the persecution of its adherents. Consider the following examples of the tenacity of the followers of the Bible in preserving its text in the midst of persecution.

"Voltaire, the noted French infidel who died in 1778, said that in one hundred years from his time Christianity would be swept from existence and passed into history. But what has happened? Voltaire has passed into history, while the circulation of the Bible continues to increase in almost all parts of the world, carrying blessing wherever it goes. For example, the English Cathedral in Zanzibar is built on the site of the Old Slave Market, and the Communion Table stands on the very spot where the whipping-post once stood! The world abounds with such instances....As one has truly said, 'We might as well put our shoulder to the burning wheel of the sun, and try to stop it on its flaming course, as attempt to stop the circulation of the Bible' "[4]

There is a historical irony about the Voltaire matter. Fifty years after his death, the Geneva Bible Society used Volatire's house and printing press to print hundreds of Bibles. Further, 200 years after Voltaire's death, Christianity is still not extinct.

In A.D. 303 the Roman emperor Diocletian wrote an imperial letter ordering (1) the destruction of all Christian churches, (2) the burning of all Christian Scriptures, and (3) the loss of civil liberties by all professing Christians. That did not stop the spread of Christianity or the proclamation of God's revelation in the Bible. Constantine, the Roman emperor who succeeded Diocletian, converted to Christianity and eventually ordered 50 copies of the Scriptures to be produced by the best scribes at government expense.

The Scriptures have also survived criticism. No other book has been subjected to such thorough criticism as has been leveled at the Bible. Yet the Bible is equal to that challenge. It can withstand the most rigorous criticism imaginable. H. L. Hastings (as quoted by John Lea) comments:

"Infidels for eighteen hundred years have been refuting and overthrowing this book, and yet it stands today as solid as a rock. Its circulation increases, and it is more loved and cherished and read today than ever before. Infidels, with all their assaults, make about as much impression on this book as a man with a tack hammer would on the Pyramids of Egypt. When the French monarch proposed the persecution of the Christians in his dominion, an old statesmen and warrior said to him, 'Sire, the Church of God is an anvil that has worn out many hammers.' So the hammers of infidels have been pecking away at this book for ages, but the hammers are worn out, and the anvil still endures. If this book had not been the book of God, men would have destroyed it long ago. Emperors and popes, kings and priests, princes and rulers have all tried their hand at it; they die and the book still lives."[5]

Gutenberg, who was one of the inventors of the art of printing.

The testimony is clear. Time passes, but the Bible remains a dramatic testimony to the keeping power of God for His revelation. Rulers come and go. The Bible remains. Critics come and go. The Bible remains. The prophet Isaiah, speaking 2,700 years ago, declared:

"All flesh is grass, and all its loveliness is like the flower of the field. The grass withers, the flower fades, when the breath of the Lord blows upon it; surely the people are grass. The grass withers, the flower fades, but the word of our God stands forever."[6]

The Wonder of Its Scientific Accuracy

One of the wonders of the Bible is its remarkable scientific accuracy, even though the Bible is not primarily a scientific book. Whenever the biblical writers touch on scientific matters in their narratives, their observations about nature, man, history and society are accurate and remarkably free of the ancient and unsophisticated scientific inaccuracies of their contemporaries. The mythologies pervasive in ancient cultures are missing from the records of the Old and New Testaments. Charles Woodruff Shields observed, "Although scientifically the Hebrews did not make the advances that the Assyrians or Egyptians or Greeks did, nevertheless, the Hebrews were free from the grotesque absurdity which disfigures the astronomy or geology of their contemporaries as found in the sacred books of the east or even in the more artistic mythology of the Greeks."[7]

There are vast differences between the historically sound accounts of creation found in the Bible and the unscientific, absurd accounts of crea-

Explicit epla pa. Incipit plogus in scdam
Post actam epistolam ad co.
ad corinthijs penitentiam
consolatoriam scribit eis epi=
stolam apostol9 a troade
per thitu: et collaudes eos hortat ad
meliora: tristatos quide eos sed eme=
datos ostendens. Explicit plogus.
Incipit scda. epla. Ad corinthios.

Aulus apostolus
cristi ihesu per volu=
tatem dei et thimo=
teus frater: ecclesie
dei que est corinthi
nu omnibz sanctis q
sunt in uniusa achaia. Gratia vobi
et pax a deo patre nostro z dno ihesu
cristo. Benedict9 deus et pater dni nri
ihesu cristi pater misericordiaz z deus
totius dsolationis. qui dsolat nos
in omni tribulatione nostra: ut possi=
mus et ipsi consolari eos qui in omni
pressura sunt per exhortatione qua ex
hortamur et ipi a deo: quonia sicut ha
bundant passiones cristi in nobis ita
et per cristu habudat dsolatio nostra.
Siue aute tribulamur pro ura exhor=
tatione et salute. siue dsolamur pro
vestra consolatione. siue exhortamur
pro ura exhortatione z salute. que op=
ratur tolleratia earudem passionum
quas et nos patimur. ut spes nostra
firma sit pro vobis: scientes quoni
am sicut socij passionu estis. sic eritis
z cosolationis. Non eni volum9 igno=
rare vos fratres de tribulatione nra
que fada est i asia: quonia supra mo
du grauati sum9 supra virtute. ita ut
tederet nos etia viuere. Sed ipi in no=
bismetipsis resposum mortis habui=
mus. ut non sim9 fidentes in nobis sed
in deo q suscitat mortuos: qui de tatis

periculis nos eripuit et eruit: in quem
speram9 quonia et adhuc eripiet ad
iuuantibz et vobis in oratone pro no=
bis. ut ex multaz personis faciez eius
que in nobis est donationis per multos
gratie agant pro nobis. Nam glori=
a nostra hec est testimoniu consciencie
nostre: cp in simplicitate cordis et sin
ceritate dei et non in sapientia carnali
sed in gratia dei conuersati sum9 in hoc
mudo. habundantius aute ad vos.
No eni alia scribimus vobis cp que
legistis et cognouistis. Spero autem
cp usqz i fine agnoscetis. sicut z cogno
uistis nos ex parte: qa gloria vestra
sum9 sicut et vos nostra i die dni nri
ihesu cristi. Et hac confidetia volui pri
us venire ad vos ut secudam gratia
haberetis. et per vos transire in mace
doniam et iteru a macedonia venire
ad vos et a vobis deduci in iudeam.
Cu ergo hoc voluissem: nuquid leui
tate usus sum. Aut que cogito scdm
carne cogito ut sit apud me est et non?
Fideles aute deus quia sermo noster
qui fuit apud vos. non est in illo e z no
sed est in illo est. Dei eni fili9 ihesus cri
stus qui in vobis per nos pdicat9 est
per me z siluanu z thimotheu no fuit
in illo est et no: sed est i illo fuit. Quot
quot eni promissiones dei sunt i illo e.
Ideo et per ipm amen deo ad gloria
nram. Qui aut dfirmat nos vobiscu
i cristo. z q unxit nos de9: et qui signa
uit nos et dedit pign9 spiric9 in cordi
bus nris. Ego aut teste du inuoco in
anima meam cp parcens vobis non
veni ultra corinthum. non quia do
minamur fidei vestre sed adiutores su
mus gaudij vestri: na fide statis. cap ij.

Statui aut hocipsum apud me:
ne iterum in tristicia venire ad

tion popular at the same time in other cultures.

The Babylonian mythological account of creation is a good example of the grotesque views current in the ancient world. The account below is quoted from a commentary by religions expert John B. Noss:

"...according to another legend..., the present world order was formed after a primeval conflict between the dragons of darkness and chaos, led by the bird-god Zu (or in other accounts by Tiamat) and the gods of light and order, headed by Ninurta, the war-god. But the Babylonian priests rewrote whatever materials they inherited, and they made Marduk both the hero of the struggle against chaos and the creator of the world and of man. Their story began with Apsu, the god of fresh water, and Tiamat, the dragon of the unbounded salt water (chaos). By their intermingling, this pair over a period of years produced the gods, but the youthful gods were so lively and boisterous that Apsu could not rest and resolved to destroy them, against the wish of Tiamat.

> Apsu, opening his mouth,
> Said unto resplendent Tiamat:
> "Their ways are verily loathsome unto me.
> By day I find no relief, nor repose by night.
> I will destroy, I will wreck their ways.
> That quiet may be restored. Let us have rest!"
> As soon as Tiamat heard this,
> She was wroth and called out to her husband.
> She cried out aggrieved, as she raged all alone,
> Injecting woe into her mood:
> "What? Should we destroy that which we have built?"
> Their ways are most troublesome, but let us attend kindly!

"But before Apsu could execute his plan, he was destroyed by Ea, who got wind of it, whereupon Tiamat resolved on avenging him. She created monsters to be her allies, and both Anu and Ea fled before her. Not until Marduk, assured by the gods that he would be their chief, came forth to meet her in combat was she halted.

> Then advanced Tiamat and Marduk, counselor of the gods;
> To the combat they marched, they drew nigh to battle,
> The lord spread out his net and caught her,
> The storm wind that was behind him, he let loose in her face.
> When Tiamat opened her mouth to its widest,
> He drove in the evil wind, that she could not close her lips...
> He made her powerless, he destroyed her life;
> He cast down her body and stood upon it.

"After next subduing the monsters she had arrayed against him, Marduk turned back to Tiamat and split her open like a shellfish into halves. With one half he made the canopy which holds back the waters that are above the heavens; with the other half he formed the covering which lies above the waters under the earth. He constructed stations for the gods in the heavens. With Ea's help he made man from the blood of the god Kingsu, Tiamat's ally and second husband. Seeing what he had done, the delighted gods bestowed on him many titles as their undisputed leader and king."[8]

The above account contrasts sharply with both the scientific evidence regarding creation and with the biblical account, which tells of an all-powerful, eternal Creator who created the heavens and the earth from

The Roman emperor Diocletian in A.D. 303 ordered all copies of the Scriptures to be destroyed. His efforts to rid the world of the Bible were fruitless, for the next Roman emperor, Constantine, became a Christian and ordered his scribes to prepare 50 new copies at his own expense.

A page from the Gutenberg Bible from the year 1445.

19

nothing. The Genesis account of creation, while not a scientific narrative in itself, is completely harmonious with scientific evidence.

The great theologian James Orr observed:

"No stronger proof could be afforded of the truth and sublimity of the biblical account of the origin of things than is given by the comparison of the narrative of creation in Genesis 1—2:4, with the mythological cosmogonies and theogonies found in other religions."[9]

As another example of the harmony between science and Scripture, we turn to Noah's ark. The dimensions of Noah's ark as revealed in the Bible are completely credible when compared to barges and large ocean-going vessels in use in this present century. But the Babylonian account of the flood describes an ark that would be completely unseaworthy and scientifically impossible. F. A. Filby comments:

"Noah's ark was the largest sea-going vessel ever built, until the late nineteenth century when giant metal ships were first constructed. The ark was approximately 450 feet by 75 feet; but as late as 1858 'the largest vessel of her type in the world was the P & O liner Himalaya, 240 feet by 35 feet...' In that year, Isambard K. Brunel produced the Great Eastern, 692 feet by 83 feet by 30 feet of approximately 19,000 tons...five times the tonnage of any ship then afloat. So vast was Brunel's leap that even forty years later in an age of fierce competition the largest liners being built were still smaller than the Great Eastern....' The Babylonian account which speaks of the ark as a cube betrays complete ignorance. Such a vessel would spin slowly around. But the biblical ratios leave nothing to be desired. These ratios are important from the point of view of stability, of pitching and rolling. The ratio of length to breadth, 300 to 50, is 6 to 1. Taking the mean of six present-day ships of approximately the same size, selected from six different shipping lines, we obtain, as an example, a ratio of 8.1 to 1. The giant liner Queen Elizabeth has a ratio of 8.6 to 1 while the Canberra has 8.2 to 1. But these vessels were designed for speed; the ark was not. Some of the giant tankers have ratios around 7 to 1. Still more interesting are the figures for the Great Britain, designed by I. K. Brunel in 1844. Her dimensions were 322 feet by 51 feet by 32½ feet, so that the ratios are almost exactly those of the ark. Brunel had the accumulated knowledge of generations of shipbuilders to draw upon. The ark was the first of its kind."[10]

Whenever the Bible touches on areas of science (for example, in discussing the creation, the flood, etc.), it does it accurately. No scientific observation in the Bible contradicts known scientific evidence. We must emphasize, however, that the Bible is not a scientific textbook; it is not intended to be understood only by a scientific elite. It is not written in scientific vocabulary. It is primarily a book about God's revelation to and relationship with humankind. The language of Scripture is neither scientific nor unscientific, but *nonscientific*. It is the language of everyday conversation, the language of common communication.

Two pitfalls should be avoided concerning the Bible and science. The first is the tendency to accuse the Bible of being unscientific for using nonscientific language in an ordinary way. An example often pointed to by critics is the biblical account of the sun "standing still" in the sky during Joshua's long day. The critic failed to take common language conventions into consideration. How many critics hear their local television weather report state that "the rotation of the earth on its axis will move

The Gospell of.S. Mathew. Fo .j.

¶ The First Chapter.

Tys is the boke off the generacion off Jhesus christ the sonne of David/the sone also of Abraham. Abraham begat Isaac: Isaac begat Jacob: Jacob begat Judas and hys brethren: Judas begat phares and zara offthamar: Phares begat Esrom: Esrom begat Aram: Aram begat Aminadab: Aminadab begat Naasson: Naasson begat Salmon: Salmon begat Boos of Rahab: Boos begat Obed of Ruth: Obed begat Jesse: Jesse begat David the kynge: ¶ David the kynge begat Solomō/of her that was the wyfe of Vry: Solomon begat Roboam: Roboam begat Abia: Abia begat Asa: Asa begat Josaphat: Josaphat begat Joram: Joram begat Osias: Osias begat Joatham: Joatham begat Achas: Achas begat Ezechias:

A ij

A representative page from the Tyndale New Testament, printed in 1526. This was one of the first stages in the development of the Bible in the English language.

our area out of the path of direct sunlight at 5:45 this evening"? On the contrary, the common report is that "Sunset tonight will be at 5:45." The critic has a tendency to place greater restrictions on the language of the Bible than he does on himself and those around him. To do so is untenable and, ultimately, unscientific.

(2) Another pitfall can be seen in the tendency of overzealous Christians to pepper the biblical text with complicated technical and scientific concepts that are not contextually present. That is, they are not really there in the context of whatever biblical statement is being discussed. Such enthusiastic defenders of the Bible may see scientific pre-figurements of atom bombs, hydrogen bombs, helicopters, germ warfare, and so on. We

The Aitken Bible, the first printing of the King James Bible in America, the only publication of the Bible authorized by Congress. This page faces the beginning of Genesis and contains the Congressional recommendation that this edition be printed.

The first page of the book of Genesis in the Aitken Bible. It was printed in 1782.

must remember that the Bible is a record of God's dealings with humankind as well as a promise of God's future blessings in the eternal kingdom for those who love Him. Such twentieth-century prefigurements are not really probably from the context of the Bible passages under consideration.

Even though the Bible is not a scientific textbook and is not written in scientific language, it is wonderful that in all of its particular observations concerning science, it is accurate, faithful to scientific evidence, and in dramatic contrast to other primitive and mythological religious writings. The apostle Paul reminded us that the God of the Bible "who made the world and all things in it, since He is Lord of heaven and earth, does not dwell in temples made with hands; neither is He served by human hands, as though He needed anything, since He Himself gives to all life and breath and all things" (Acts 17:24, 25).

The Wonder of Its Frankness

An amazing feature of the Bible is the frankness with which it deals with

21

the frailties of the people of God and even with the shortcomings of its own authors. The Bible paints a realistic portrait of its characters, resisting the temptation to mythologize or perfect them. For example, the book of Genesis reveals that even Noah, a great man of God who saved the remnant of humanity from the Great Flood, was once found in a drunken stupor: "Then Noah began farming and planted a vineyard. And he drank of the wine and became drunk, and uncovered himself inside his tent. And Ham, the father of Canaan, saw the nakedness of his father, and told his two brothers outside. But Shem and Japheth took a garment and laid it upon both their shoulders and walked backward and covered the nakedness of their father; and their faces were turned away, so that they

Not only were copies of the Bible destroyed by haters of Christianity, but many Christians paid for their faith with their lives.

did not see their father's nakedness" (Genesis 9:20-23).

Abraham, called the "father of the faithful," also had his lapses, for example: "And Abraham said of Sarah his wife, 'She is my sister.' So Abimelech king of Gerar sent and took Sarah. But God came to Abimelech in a dream of the night, and said to him, 'Behold, you are a dead man because of the woman whom you have taken, for she is married.'. . .Then Abimelech called Abraham and said to him, 'What have you done to us? And how have I sinned against you, that you have brought on me and on my kingdom a great sin? You have done to me things that ought not to be done'" (Genesis 20:2,3,9).

We see in 2 Samuel 11 that David, the man after God's own heart, was a murderer and an adulterer. Verses 3, 4, 14 and 15 tell us: "So David sent and inquired about the woman. And one said, 'Is this not Bathsheba, the daughter of Eliam, the wife of Uriah the Hittite?' And David sent messengers and took her, and when she came to him, he lay with her; and when she had purified herself from her uncleanness, she returned to her house. . . .Now it came about in the morning that David wrote a letter to Joab, and sent it by the hand of Uriah. And he had written in the letter, saying, 'Place Uriah in the front line of the fiercest battle and withdraw from him, so that he may be struck down and die.'"

22

The disciples of Jesus Christ, the pillars of the Christian church, often stumbled, for example: "'And you shall say to the owner of the house, "The Teacher says to you, 'Where is the guest room in which I may eat the Passover with My disciples?'"'... And there arose also a dispute among them as to which one of them was regarded to be greatest" (Luke 22:11,24).

The apostle Paul argued with his companion, Barnabas: "And after some days Paul said to Barnabas, 'Let us return and visit the brethren in every city in which we proclaimed the word of the Lord, and see how they are.' And Barnabas was desirous of taking John, called Mark, along with them also. But Paul kept insisting that they should not take him along who had deserted them in Pamphylia and had not gone with them to the work.

The Wycliffe Bible Translators is one of the organizations committed to translating the Bible into every language known to man. They have already translated the Scriptures into over 1600 languages! Yet the task continues for there are between 3,000 and 5,000 languages and dialects that are spoken in the world.

And there arose such a sharp disagreement that they separated from one another, and Barnabas took Mark with him and sailed away to Cyprus" (Acts 15:36-39).

The fact that the personalities in the Bible are flawed does not detract from the biblical message: it is the holiness of the Lord God that the Bible proclaims, not the perfection of His followers and prophets. Yet the greatest personality revealed in the Bible, the one of whom in some sense the whole Bible speaks, is described as being without sin, as perfect and holy as His Father. This perfect one is Jesus Christ our Lord. Bible expositor Wilbur Smith declared:

"Fifteen million minutes of life on this earth, in the midst of a wicked and corrupt generation—every thought, every deed, every purpose, every work, privately and publicly, from the time He opened His baby eyes until He expired on the cross, were all approved of God. Never once did our Lord have to confess any sin, for He had no sin."[11]

The frankness of the Bible is refreshing. The faults of its characters (except for the sinless Son of God) are not overlooked. That frankness is another wonderful characteristic.

The Wonder of Predictive Prophecy

One of the most incredible features of the Bible is its predictive prophecies.

23

In no other books do we find the wealth of prophecies, clearly made years before their fulfillment, and all accurately fulfilled in history.

The biblical prophet was a spokesman for God to the people. He not only predicted future events in God's plan, he also exhorted and admonished the people according to the directives of the Lord. His task of exhortation, in fact, occupied more of his time and words than did his prophesying of future events. It is with predictive prophecy, however, that we are here concerned.

Predictive prophecy was given to inform humankind of the nature and attributes of the Lord God and of His goals for His creation.

Moses coming down from Mt. Sinai with the tablets of stone containing the Ten Commandments.

One of the oldest writing materials was clay. These clay tablets from Ebla are an example of ancient writing. The signs were etched in the soft clay with a metal stylus, and when the clay hardened the tablets could be kept for a long time.

"Remember the former things long past, for I am God, and there is no other; I am God, and there is no one like Me, declaring the end from the beginning and from ancient times things which have not been done, saying, 'My purpose will be established, and I will accomplish all My good pleasure.'"[12]

"I declared the former things long ago and they went forth from My mouth, and I proclaimed them. Suddenly I acted, and they came to pass. Because I know that you are obstinate, and your neck is an iron sinew, and your forehead bronze, therefore I declared them to you long ago, before they took place I proclaimed them to you, lest you should say, 'My idol has done them, and my graven image and my molten image have commanded them.'"[13]

There are dozens of examples of fulfilled prophecy to which we could point in both the Old Testament and the New. The most important propecies, some fulfilled and some yet to be fulfilled, concern Jesus Christ, the most important person in the Bible. As representative of the fulfilled prophecies in the Bible we will examine some concerning the first coming of God's Son, Jesus, who was made flesh 2,000 years ago.[14]

The Old Testament contains dozens of prophecies about the coming Savior and deliverer of God's people, the Messiah of Israel. Christ's work of salvation for humankind through His sacrifice on the cross fulfilled many

of them. Some still wait their fulfillment for the Second Coming, when the Lord returns from heaven in judgment and victory.

One set of Old Testament prophecies about the Messiah has to do with His family lineage. Those prophecies, given long before Jesus was born, indicate that His lineage would be through the royal house of Israel. That is something over which Jesus Himself could have no control: He could not manipulate the fulfillment of such prophecies in Himself. The one coming would come from the line of Abraham: "And I will bless those who bless you, and the one who curses you I will curse. And in you all the families of the earth shall be blessed" (Genesis 12:3).

Abraham had two sons, Isaac and Ishmael. The Bible predicts that the Messiah was to come through the line of Isaac: "But God said to Abraham, 'Do not be distressed because of the lad and your maid; whatever Sarah tells you, listen to her, for through Isaac your descendants shall be named'" (Genesis 21:12).

Of Isaac's two sons, Jacob and Esau, the Messiah was to come from Jacob's line: "Your descendants shall also be like the dust of the earth and you shall spread out to the west and to the east and to the north and to the south; and in you and in your descendants shall all the families of the earth be blessed" (Genesis 28:14); "I see him, but not now; I behold him, but not near; a star shall come forth from Jacob, and a scepter shall rise from Israel, and shall crush through the forehead of Moab, and tear down all the sons of Sheth" (Numbers 24:17).

Out of Jacob's 12 sons the Messiah was to descend from the line of Judah: "The scepter shall not depart from Judah, nor the ruler's staff from between his feet, until Shiloh comes, and to him shall be the obedience of the peoples" (Genesis 49:10).

Jesse, of the tribe of Judah, had eight sons; the Bible predicts that the Messiah would come from his son David: "And your house and your kingdom shall endure before Me forever; your throne shall be established forever" (2 Samuel 7:16); "'Behold the days are coming,' declares the Lord, 'when I shall raise up for David a righteous Branch; and He will reign as king and act wisely and do justice and righteousness in the land. In His days Judah will be saved, and Israel will dwell securely; and this is His name by which He will be called, "The Lord our righteousness"'" (Jeremiah 23:5,6).

His reign is confirmed by Isaiah: "Then a shoot will spring from the stem of Jesse, and a branch from his roots will bear fruit. And the Spirit of the Lord will rest on Him, the spirit of wisdom and understanding, the spirit of counsel and strength, the spirit of knowledge and the fear of the Lord. And He will delight in the fear of the Lord, and He will not judge by what His eyes see, nor make a decision by what His ears hear; but with righteousness He will judge the poor, and decide with fairness for the afflicted of the earth; and He will strike the earth with the rod of His mouth, and with the breath of His lips He will slay the wicked. Also righteousness will be the belt about His loins, and faithfulness the belt about His waist" (Isaiah 11:1-5).

Thirty times in the New Testament Jesus Christ is said to be descended from David. Three of those statements are: "The book of the genealogy of Jesus Christ, the son of David, the son of Abraham" (Matthew 1:1); "And when He began His ministry, Jesus Himself was about thirty years of age, being supposedly the son of Joseph, the son of Eli...the son of Melea, the son of Menna, the son of Mattatha, the son of Nathan, the son of David" (Luke 3:23,31); and "concerning His Son, who was born of a descendant of David according to the flesh" (Romans 1:3).

This abundance of predictive detail was beyond the control of any human being and is indicative of the inspiration of the Scriptures and the Messiahship of Jesus of Nazareth.

Another set of Scriptures concerns the birthplace of the Messiah. In the Old Testament we find the prophecy concerning the location of the coming Messiah's birth: "Now muster yourselves in troops, daughter of troops; they have laid siege against us; with a rod they will smite the judge of Israel on the cheek. But as for you, Bethlehem Ephrathah, too little to be among the clans of Judah, from you One will go forth for Me to be ruler in Israel. His goings forth are from long ago, from the days of eternity. Therefore, He will give them up until the time when she who is in labor has borne a child. Then the remainder of His brethren will return to the sons of Israel" (Micah 5:1-3). The savior was not to be born in the large capital city, Jerusalem, but in the tiny village of Bethlehem. Once that prophecy in Micah was given, no other city in the world could be the legitimate birthplace of the Messiah. Jesus of Nazareth fulfilled that Old Testament prophecy. Matthew 2:1 states clearly that Jesus was born in Bethlehem: "Now after Jesus was born in Bethlehem of Judea in the days of Herod the king..." The prophecy was even so explicit as to designate Bethlehem Ephrathah, rather than Bethlehem in Zebulun. Ephrathah was a particular district within which the Bethlehem of Jesus' birth was located: "And the name of the man was Elimelech, and the name of his wife, Naomi; and the names of his two sons were Mahlon and Chilion, Ephrathites of Bethlehem in Judah" (Ruth 1:2).

Those two sets of verses are just a small representation of the many predictive prophecies found in the Bible that have been fulfilled according to God's divine plan. Predictive prophecy is a unique and wonderful feature of the Bible.

These clay tablets, found in northern Syria, are from the kingdom of Ebla, 2250 B.C. Some 15,000 tablets have been discovered which shows writing played an important role in the ancient world long before the time of Moses.

The Wonder of Its Christ-Centeredness

Another unique and wonderful feature of the Bible is its Christ-centeredness. The Bible, from beginning to end, in both Old and New Testaments, is a testimony to Jesus Christ, the "Son of Man" and the Lord of Glory. After the resurrection, Jesus Christ Himself explained how the Scriptures center on Him:

"O foolish men and slow of heart to believe in all that the prophets have spoken! Was it not necessary for the Christ to suffer these things and to enter into His glory? And beginning with Moses and with all the prophets, He explained to them the things concerning Himself in all the Scriptures."[15]

Even before His death, Jesus Christ pointed out the Christ-centeredness of the Scriptures. When the Jews who continually harassed Jesus challenged His authority, He responded:

"You search the Scriptures, because you think that in them you have eternal life; and it is these that bear witness of Me; and you are unwilling to come to Me, that you may have life."[16]

The Old Testament records the preparation for the coming of Christ: "A voice is calling, 'Clear the way for the Lord in the wilderness; make smooth in the desert a highway for our God'" (Isaiah 40:3). The theme toward which the Old Testament is pointing is the establishment of the kingdom of God through the reign of the Messiah, the Christ. The Old Testament looks forward to His coming and tells us what it will be like.

Genesis: Adam is the "figure of him that was to come" (Rom. 5:14)
>   the posterity of the woman was to be Christ, who would bruise and crush the head of the serpent (Gen. 3:15)
>   the blood of Abel, the righteous man, is compared to the blood shed on the cross (Heb. 12:24)
>   Melchizedek is said to be like unto the Son of God (Gen. 14:18-20; Heb. 7:1-10)
>   Isaac, the son loved of his father, was offered as a sacrifice at the very spot where the only-begotten Son of God was to be put to

The entrance gate to the city and the royal palace of Ebla. The clay tablets were discovered in the royal archives.

>   death (Gen. 22; II Chron. 3:1)

Shiloh is the Sovereign from the tribe of Judah (Gen. 49:10)

Exodus: the Passover Lamb (Exodus 12; John 1:29; I Cor. 5:7)
>   the manna, miraculous bread sent down from heaven (Exodus 16; John 6:31-33)
>   the smitten rock, which "was Christ" (Exodus 17:1-7; I Cor. 10:4)

Leviticus: the bleeding sacrifices, picture of the cross (Heb. 9:12-14; 10:1-4, 11-14)
>   Aaron, type of Christ, our High Priest (Heb. 7:11-28)
>   the veil, symbol of the flesh of Jesus torn and broken on Calvary (Heb. 10:20)

Numbers: Aaron's rod, parable of the resurrection of the Lord (Num. 17:1-11)
>   the red heifer, another prefiguration of the purifying sacrifice (Num. 19; Heb. 9:13)
>   the brazen serpent, representing Christ on the cross (Num. 21:4-9; John 3:14-16), etc.

Going over to the Psalms, we see the details in the portrait of the Messiah sketched in all the way through them.

>   Psalm 2:   Jehovah and His Anointed
>   8:   the Son of Man and His humiliation

(Above) A potsherd bearing Egyptian hieroglyphics was also found at Ebla. The name of the pharaoh mentioned on the potsherd makes dating of this discovery possible.

(Below) One of the factors used to determine the age of manuscripts is the letter-type. Minuscule or lower case writing replaced the uncial, or upper case letters, in the ninth century A.D. This is an example of a Carolinian minuscule in the Psalter of Corbie from the ninth century.

16:	the Beloved delivered to the place of the dead
22:	the sufferings on the cross
69:	the insults and the gall and vinegar
72:	the King of peace
110:	the Lord glorified

Among the prophets, Isaiah has been called the evangelist of the Old Testament. He indeed does present to us:

Isaiah 7:14:	Immanuel, born of a virgin
9:6:	the Son given, the Mighty God, the Prince of Peace
11:1-10:	the shoot out of the stock of Jesse, clothed with the Spirit who "shall rest" upon Him
40:1-10:	the God who was to come
40:11:	the Shepherd of the sheep
42:1-4; 49:1-7:	the Servant of Jehovah
53:	the Man of sorrows
61:1-2:	the Anointed of God, the Emancipator
63:1-6:	the Judge

Let us mention, finally, the prediction of Zechariah and its extraordinary precision:

Zechariah 3:1-5:	the Angel of Jehovah, the Advocate
3:9-10; 4:7:	the Cornerstone
6:12-13:	the Branch of the Lord, at once Priest and King
9:9:	the humble King, mounted on an ass
11:7-14:	the Shepherd sold for thirty pieces of silver
12:10:	the One whom they pierced
13:7:	the Shepherd smitten for the sheep
14:3-4:	Jehovah triumphant

The New Testament tells of His first coming and anticipates His Second Coming. John 1:1, 14, 29 records the fulfillment of the Old Testament prophecies concerning the first coming of the Messiah:

"In the beginning was the Word, and the Word was with God, and the Word was God.... And the Word became flesh, and dwelt among us, and we beheld His glory, glory as of the only begotten from the Father, full of grace and truth.... The next day [John the Baptist] saw Jesus coming to him, and said, 'Behold, the Lamb of God who takes away the sin of the world!'"[17]

Before His death Jesus Christ described to His disciples the necessity for His death, burial, and resurrection in order to accomplish redemption for the world. But He did not stop there. He also described to them His Second Coming, with glory, power, and judgment at the end of the age:

"For just as the lightning comes from the east, and flashes even to the west, so shall the coming of the Son of Man be....and then the sign of the Son of Man will appear in the sky, and then all the tribes of the earth will mourn, and they will see the Son of Man coming on the clouds of the sky, with power and great glory. And He will send forth His angels with a great trumpet and they will gather together His elect from the four winds, from one end of the sky to the other."[18]

The Old Testament records the preparation for the coming of the Messiah. The gospels record the coming of the Messiah, Jesus Christ our Lord. The book of Acts records the progagation of the gospel (the good news) concerning Jesus Christ. The epistles (letters) explain the gospel and its implications for our lives. The book of Revelation anticipates and describes the Second Coming of Jesus Christ and the establishment of His eternal

On the right: Before books with pages came to be used, like the one you are reading right now, book-scrolls were often used. Strips of papyrus sheets or of parchment were fastened together, so that a scroll was about 20 to 35 feet long (6 to 10 meters). Scrolls of more than 140 feet (over 40 meters) have also been found! Even today, the book-scrolls have their place in Jewish religious services.

kingdom. From beginning to end, the Bible glorifies Jesus Christ and centers on Him. Its Christ-centeredness is one of its wonderful features.

The Wonder of Its Intellectual Integrity

One of the Bible's most wonderful features is the intellectual integrity it inspires in its readers. Although it was composed between two and four thousand years ago, it still has the power to challenge intelligent men and women to develop their full intellectual capabilities in studying its rich teachings and history. It can stand the test of the most rigorous intellectual assault and emerge as strong as before. Those who have dedicated their lives to understanding and appreciating the Scriptures have never been disappointed.

One example is that of the late Dr. Robert Dick Wilson. His intellectual achievements have been chronicled in another of our books as follows:

"The story of Dr. Robert Dick Wilson stands as a remarkable testimony to the reliability of the Bible. Wilson's scholarship, in many ways still unsurpassed, gave the world compelling evidence that the Old Testament is an accurate and trustworthy document. Robert Dick Wilson was born in 1856 in Pennsylvania. In 1886 Wilson received the Doctor's degree. He continued his training at Western Theological Seminary in Pittsburgh, followed by two years in Germany at the University of Berlin.

Section from the Gospel according to Matthew (chapter 10) in uncial script (Bodleian Library, Oxford).

"Upon his arrival in Germany, Professor Wilson made a decision to dedicate his life to the study of the Old Testament. He recounted his decision, 'I was twenty-five then; and I judged from the life of my ancestors that I should live to be seventy; so that I should have forty-five years to work. I divided the period into three parts. The first fifteen years I would devote to the study of the languages necessary. For the second fifteen I was going to devote myself to the study of the text of the Old Testament; and I reserved the last fifteen years for the work of writing the results of my previous studies and investigations, so as to give them to the world.' Dr. Wilson's plans were carried out almost to the very year he had projected, and his scholastic accomplishments were truly amazing.

"As a student in seminary he would read the New Testament in nine different languages including a Hebrew translation which he had memorized syllable for syllable! Wilson also memorized large portions of the Old Testament in the original Hebrew. Incredible as it may seem, Robert Dick Wilson mastered forty-five languages and dialects. Dr. John Walvoord, president of Dallas Theological Seminary, called Dr. Wilson 'probably the outstanding authority on ancient languages of the Middle East.'

"Dr. Wilson commented on his scholastic achievements, relating why he devoted himself to such a monumental task: 'Most of our students used to go to Germany, and they heard professors give lectures which were the results of their own labours. I went there to study so that there would be no professor on earth that could lay down the law for me, or say anything without my being able to investigate the evidence on which he said it.

"'Now I consider that what was necessary in order to investigate the evidence was, first of all, to know the languages in which the evidence is given. So I...determined that I would learn all the languages that throw light upon the Hebrew, and also the languages into which the Bible had been translated down to A.D. 600, so that I could investigate the text myself.

"'Having done this I claim to be an expert. I defy any man to make an attack upon the Old Testament on the ground of evidence that I cannot investigate. I can get the facts if they are linguistic. If you know any language that I do not know, I will learn it.'

"Wilson challenged other so-called 'experts' in the Old Testament field demanding that they prove their qualifications before making statements concerning its history and text. 'If a man is called an expert, the first thing to be done is to establish the fact that he is such. One expert may be worth more than a million other witnesses that are not experts. Before a man has the right to speak about the history, the language, and the paleography of the Old Testament, the Christian church has the right to demand that such a man establish his ability to do so.'

"Dr. Wilson met his own challenge. For 46 years Wilson had devoted himself to this great task of studying the Old Testament, carefully investigating the evidence that had a bearing upon its historical reliability. Based upon his credentials he was in a better position to speak as an expert than any other man. His findings drove him to the firm conviction that 'in the Old Testament we have a true historical account of the history of the Israelite people.'

"As a professor at Princeton Dr. Wilson won international fame as a scholar and defender of the historic Christian faith. The emphasis of Professor Wilson's teaching was to give his students 'such an intelligent faith in the Old Testament scriptures that they will never doubt them as long as they live.' He tried to 'show them that there is reasonable ground for belief in the history of the Old Testament' "[19] (Josh McDowell and Don Stewart, *Answers,* dedication).

A more contemporary example of a person whose intellectual pursuits were spurred on by his devotion to the Scriptures is the noted Christian scholar, Dr. E. M. Blaiklock. He writes:

"I claim to be an historian. My approach to Classics is historical. And I tell you that the evidence for the life, the death, and the resurrection of Christ is better authenticated than most of the facts of ancient history,

The Codex Vaticanus (see picture) is one of the most valuable manuscripts of the Greek Bible. Written about the middle of the 4th century A.D., it contains the Greek translation of the Old Testament, the Greek New Testament and most of the apocryphal books. Some scholars think it is one of the 50 copies of the Bible which emperor Constantine had ordered at his own expense.

which I taught for forty-two years as a university teacher with some confidence. I said that [Christ] was quite different from anyone I had ever seen. And as a figure of history, Christ is precisely that. Four small books of simple Greek, called the Gospels, picture a Person who was not the product of His times, but remote from human conception or expectation—so remote that His own men never fully understood Him, until an astounding event transformed them, enlightened them, and so launched them on the world that the dozen of them infiltrated the Roman Empire in a generation. Their successors beat that Empire to its knees in three centuries.

"Here are the alternatives. Either four men, only one of them with any education in the liberal sense of the word, invented the Character who altered the whole course of history, or they wrote of One they knew or had heard about from those who knew Him, a Person so extraordinary that He could claim deity, sinlessness, all authority, and rouse no revulsion among those who long knew Him intimately and experimentally. The religious leaders, collaborators with the occupying power, so feared Him that they betrayed and murdered Him, and in so doing, like the doomed actors in an Aristotelian tragedy, loosed forces which swept the world."[20]

33

The Bible tells us we are to love the Lord our God with all our mind (Matthew 22:37). Twentieth-century men and women can use their minds, taking the Bible and evaluating it with full intellectual scrutiny. The Bible will prevail and continue to satisfy and stimulate the intellect of any who fairly investigate its claims. The wonder of the Bible's intellectual integrity is amazing.

The Wonder of Its Teachings

Another wonderful aspect of the Bible separates it from all other religious books and is a testimony to its divine origin. This is the wonder of its unique teachings. The teachings in the Bible cannot be explained as a

Before the invention of the art of printing the Bible had to be transcribed by hand. This was often done in so called "scriptoria," where a reader slowly read the text and the copyists wrote what they heard. The tremendous spread of the Christian faith during the first centuries A.D. necessitated the production of many such copies. Because of this manual work a complete Bible was a valuable book to possess.

product of the religious environment of its authors, since many of its teachings were contrary to contemporary religious thought and were hard for the Jews themselves to accept. Of many such examples we will discuss just a few representative ones.

Much of the unique teaching in the Bible centers around the personal God it reveals. Israel was surrounded by polytheistic cultures (cultures that believed in more than one God). Israel often slipped into idolatry itself. Yet its holy Scriptures, the Old Testament, betray not a word in favor of idolatry or polytheism. The Old Testament, in fact, is replete with warnings against idolatry and with condemnation of idolators. In addition, the Bible repeatedly emphasizes the monotheism (belief in one God) which is the bulwark of biblical theology. Here are two scriptural examples:

"Hear, O Israel! The Lord is our God, the Lord is one! And you shall love the Lord your God with all your heart and with all your soul and with all your might."[21]

"You are My witnesses," declares the Lord, "And My servant whom I have chosen, in order that you may know and believe Me, and understand that I am He. Before Me there was no God formed, and there will be none after Me. I, even I, am the Lord; and there is no savior besides Me"[21]

The New Testament continues the absolute monotheism of the Old Testament:

"....we know that there is no such thing as an idol in the world, and that there is no God but one. For even if there are so-called gods whether in heaven or on earth, as indeed there are many gods and many lords, yet for us there is but one God, the Father, from whom are all things, and we exist for Him; and one Lord, Jesus Christ, through whom are all things, and we exist through Him."[23]

The nature and attributes of the God of the Bible are also different from the concepts of God in cultures surrounding the Jews. The Bible reveals a God who is infinite and personal, who cares for human beings as a Father and who personifies love, respect, justice and mercy. This is in contrast to other gods of the ancient world who were to be obeyed and served out of fear rather than from loving respect. An idea of the fatherly attitude of the God of the Bible was revealed by Jesus Christ:

"And I say to you, ask, and it shall be given to you; seek, and you shall find; knock, and it shall be opened to you. For everyone who asks, receives; and he who seeks, finds; and to him who knocks, it shall be opened. Now suppose one of your fathers is asked by his son for a fish; he will not give him a snake instead of a fish, will he? Or if he is asked for an egg, he will not give him a scorpion, will he? If you then, being evil, know how to give good gifts to your children, how much more shall your Heavenly Father give the Holy Spirit to those who ask Him?"[24]

In many other religious settings God is to be obeyed in order for the faithful to receive rewards. In the Bible we are taught to obey God out of love: "If you love Me, you will keep My commandments" (John 14:15).

A final unique teaching from the Bible is the resurrection of the founder of Christianity, Jesus Christ. This teaching is a wonder since in no other religious literature do we have a resurrection that was *bodily* and that can be *tested* by the most rigorous historical methods. While many other religious traditions have ideas of spiritual or spirit resurrections (untestable hypotheses), only the Bible proclaims a bodily resurrection that passes all tests of historical reliability.

We conclude that the Bible, in both Old and New Testaments, contains teachings that are unique and wonderful in comparison to the best teachings offered in any other religious or nonreligious writings.

The Wonder of Its Life-Transforming Power

We now come to the last of the ten wonders of the Bible considered here. This wonder personalizes the facts and evidences about which we have been talking, addressing itself to the individual. This wonder is the Bible's effect on individuals. If the Bible is indeed the Word of God, it should demonstrate its ability to transform lives in harmony with its message of eternal life.

We must first note that the Bible claims that it can transform lives, filling the spiritual void within all people.

"Blessed are those who hunger and thirst for righteousness, for they shall be satisfied."[25]

"Come to Me, all who are weary and heavy-laden, and I will give you rest. Take My yoke upon you, and learn from Me, for I am gentle and humble in heart; and you shall find rest for your souls. For My yoke is easy, and My load is light."[26]

Next to Latin translations (the Vulgate) there were also early translations of the Bible into Syriac. Exactly when these Syriac translations of the Old Testament (the Peshitta) were made, is not known. Nor can tradition help us much: Some say they originated in the time of king Solomon, others point to the first centuries of the Christian church. This manuscript of Exodus 6:2-12 dates from A.D. 464 and is located in the British Museum in London.

35

"...whoever drinks of the water that I shall give him shall never thirst; but the water that I shall give him shall become in him a well of water springing up to eternal life."[27]

"You search the Scriptures, because you think that in them you have eternal life, and it is these that bear witness of Me."[28]

"I came that they might have life, and might have it abundantly. I am the good shepherd; the good shepherd lays down His life for the sheep."[29]

Christian scholar Bernard Ramm gives this perspective on the life-transforming importance of the Scriptures:

"...Whatever passes as true must have direct tangency with life and ex-

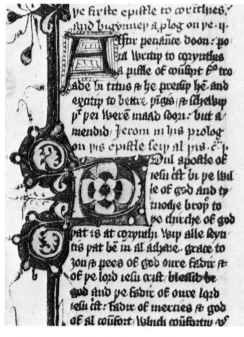

On the right: The first complete translation of the Bible into English was done by John Wycliffe (see picture below) together with John Purvey and Nicholas of Hereford in 1388. Opposition to the translation of the Bible was so great that Wycliffe's body was later dug up, burned to ashes and thrown into the river. "Wycliffe Translators of the Bible" named themselves after this courageous man. The pictured page is taken from a hand-written English translation from the end of the 14th century.

perience.... It is to be questioned if Christianity would have had the hold it has had, and does have on hundreds of thousands of people if it lacked direct tangency with life and experience even though it created such an imposing theological and philosophical edifice. Because Christianity is true it must have relevancy to every significant aspect of the universe and human experience. It must not only provide us with the materials of a great philosophy—Christian trinitarian theism—and a great theology; but it must have a relevancy or tangency to human experience."[30]

Dr. J. M. Houston, formerly of Oxford University in England, now at Regent College in Canada, tells how the Scriptures met the needs in his life:

"When I am asked the question 'Why am I a Christian?' I never have a wholly satisfying answer. Religion, according to Professor MacMurray, is what we do with our personal relationships. This view I accept. Religious experience has therefore the elements of personal will, decision, and response. Thus rational arguments in favor of Christianity are at best partial in value. They can only skate around the circumference of the situation as it is seen and lived. I cannot wholly convince the world in mental images and languages about something I feel at the much deeper level of emotion and experience. As the psalmist said: 'Oh taste and see that the Lord is good.' It is experiential rather than merely rational.

"Because Christianity is concerned essentially with that dimension we

call the 'personal,' it is living and dynamic. A Christian's awareness of his faith should grow and deepen, so that a confession of faith is at best but an interim report. As Paul confessed: 'Not that I have already obtained this or am already perfect; but I press on to make it my own, because Christ Jesus has made me his own.' (Phil. 3:12, RSV). I am conscious of the great claims made on behalf of Christianity, but I also realize how dwarfed is the response and evidence of its power in my own life. All I can say is that I know enough, in my limited experience of its winsomeness and power, to seek more of it and to value it above all else."[31]

The experience of knowing God personally through Jesus Christ is not something unique to Dr. Houston. For millions of people this life-trans-

During the time of the Reformation not only were translations made into the various national languages, but also editions of the original Hebrew and Greek texts. The first printed edition of the Greek New Testament was published in 1516; it was done by Erasmus (see picture above; he lived from about 1469 to 1536). Luther used the second printing of it for his German translation. A significant help in the study of the Bible is the comparison of texts. Christoffel Plantijn, a Flemish printer from Antwerp, published a polyglot, a Bible in several translations: on the left page, Latin and Aramaic translations of the Hebrew text, and on the right page Latin and Aramaic translations of the Greek text.

forming power is evident as they read God's revelation in the Bible and encounter the person of Jesus Christ the Savior. E. Y. Mullins observes:

"I have, for me at least, irrefutable evidence of the objective existence of the Person so moving me. When to this personal experience I add that of tens of thousands of living Christians, and an unbroken line of them back to Christ, and when I find in the New Testament a manifold record of like experiences, together with a clear account of the origin and cause of them all, my certainty becomes absolute. One of the most urgent of all duties resting upon modern Christians is to assert with clearness and vigor the certainties of Christian experience."[32]

Psychiatrist J. T. Fisher put it this way:

"If you were to take the sum total of all authoritative articles ever written by the most qualified of psychologists and psychiatrists on the subject of mental hygiene—if you were to combine them and refine them and cleave out the excess verbiage—if you were to take the whole of the meat and none of the parsley, and if you were to have these unadulterated bits of pure scientific knowledge concisely expressed by the most capable of living poets, you would have an awkward and incomplete summation of the Sermon on the Mount. And it would suffer immeasurably through comparison. For nearly two thousand years the Christian world has been holding in its hands the complete answer to its restless and fruitless yearn-

37

ings. Here...rests the blueprint for successful human life with optimism, mental health, and contentment."[33]

The wonderful, life-transforming power of the Bible is a fact. Has it changed your life?

Summary and Conclusion

The Bible is the most wonderful book ever written, as uniquely demonstrated in the aforementioned ten areas.

1. Unity.   Though the Bible contains 66 books written over a period of 1500 years by 40 different authors from different educational backgrounds, in different languages, on different continents, concerning hundreds of

The English Bible translator William Tyndale closed his eyes while being burned at the stake with the plea, "Lord, open Thou the eyes of the king of England!" The second printing of his Bible, the "Coverdale Bible," was done with the agreement of the English king.

controversial subjects, it remains a unity — one unfolding story from beginning to end.

2. Historical accuracy.   Although composed from 2000 to 4000 years ago, the Bible demonstrates itself to be historically accurate as to the people, places and events it records.

3. Indestructibility.   The Bible has survived intact throughout history despite the criticisms and persecutions. It has stood the test of time.

4. Scientific accuracy.   When dealing with areas pertaining to science, the Bible is accurate and restrained. This is in direct contrast to other ancient works which have fanciful ideas about the nature of the universe.

5. Frankness.   The Scriptures deal frankly with the sins of its characters. There is no attempt to whitewash the faults. This also is in contrast to most ancient works which attempt to put the characters in the best possible light.

6. Predictive prophecy.   Contained within the pages of Scripture are hundreds of fulfilled prophecies. No other book, ancient or modern, has anything like it.

7. Christ-centeredness.   From beginning to end, Jesus Christ is the theme of the Bible. It's all about Him.

8. Intellectual integrity.   In the 20th century educated men and women

can still study the Bible in detail and believe wholeheartedly in its message without assassinating their brains.

9. Teachings.   The teachings of the Bible are unique when compared with the surrounding nations. The writers did not borrow from their neighbors—their teachings were revealed directly by God.

10. Life-transforming power.   For the last two thousand years, the message of the Bible has been transforming lives like no other, and it is still doing it today.

The claims of a book with the remarkable credentials of the Bible deserve serious consideration. Any sincere seeker after truth should look into this

The first Bible published in America was a translation of the New Testament into the Massachusetts Indian language. It was printed in 1661. This is the title page.

A portion of the Sermon on the Mount in the gospel of Matthew, from the Massachusetts Indian translation of the New Testament.

book for answers to the ultimate questions of existence. Sir Walter Scott wrote:

> "Within that awful volume lies
> The mystery of mysteries
> Happiest they of human race
> To whom God has granted grace
> To read, to fear, to hope, to pray
> To lift the latch, and force the way;
> And better had they ne'er been born,
> Who read to doubt, or read to scorn."[34]

Now that we have seen that the Bible is not just another book, but a wonderful record of God's voice to humankind, we will go on to review the making of the Old and New Testaments. We will first delve into questions concerning the reliability of the Hebrew Scriptures. Can we really trust our Old Testament? Is the text we have today truly representative of the original? We will cover these and other interesting features about the making of the Old Testament in chapter two.

CHAPTER TWO

The Making of the Old Testament

The Hebrew Scriptures, which are the same as the 39 Old Testament books, consist of 24 books composed between 1400 B.C. and 400 B.C. They are placed into three major divisions: the Law (Torah), the Prophets (Nebhiim), and the Writings (Kethubim). They include:

The Law (or Pentateuch)

Genesis
Exodus
Leviticus
Numbers
Deuteronomy

The Prophets

A. The Former Prophets
    1. Joshua
    2. Judges
    3. 1 and 2 Samuel
    4. 1 and 2 Kings

B. The Latter Prophets
    1. Isaiah

Page 40: "How lonely sits the city that was full of people! She has become like a widow who was once great among the nations! She who was a princess among the provinces has become a forced laborer!" (Lamentations 1:1). "Jeremiah mourning over the destruction of Jerusalem" by Rembrandt.

Above: A fragment from the exceptionally well preserved Hebrew scroll of the complete book of Isaiah. The scroll is at present located in the Israel Museum in Jerusalem.

2. Jeremiah
3. Ezekiel
4. The Twelve (Hosea-Malachi)

The Writings

A. The Poetical Books
   1. Psalms
   2. Job
   3. Proverbs

B. The Five Rolls
   1. Ruth
   2. Song of Songs
   3. Ecclesiastes
   4. Lamentations
   5. Esther

C. The Historical Books
   1. Daniel
   2. Ezra-Nehemiah
   3. 1 and 2 Chronicles

The first five books of the Bible are called the Torah (or Pentateuch, the Law, the Five Books of Moses). "Torah" means teaching or instruction. The reading of the Law is a holy duty for pious Jews, who consider it as joy for the heart. In the second and fifth book of the Torah (Exodus and Deuteronomy) the Ten Commandments are written. For the Jews the Torah is the most sacred part of the Tenach (the Old Testament).

The Hebrew Bible is commonly referred to by Jewish people as the *Tenach*, a word made from the first Hebrew letter in each of the three words of the titles of the above divisions: Torah, Nebhiim, and Kethubim. The three letters, T, N, and K, combine to form Tenach.

To understand how these particular books reached their present grouping and authority in the Old Testament, we need to look at the history of the text, observing how the various books were preserved and transmitted over the centuries.

History of the Text

The books of the Old Testament, from the time of their composition, were considered special by the Jews. They were not ordinary literature or ordinary history; they were God's Word communicated to His people. Because of the high regard with which the books were held, great care was taken to preserve their texts precisely as they were originally written.

The Pentateuch identifies the priests in Israel as the ones responsible for the preservation of the Law. They were to store it beside or in the Ark of the Covenant, which was placed in the Holy of Holies in the Tabernacle and then in the Temple. The Old Testament records this command: "Take this book of the law and place it beside the ark of the covenant of the Lord your God, that it may remain there as a witness against you"[1]

The kings of Israel were required to have the Law before them as a guide in their administration of the kingdom:

"Now it shall come about when he sits on the throne of his kingdom, he shall write for himself a copy of this law on a scroll in the presence of the Levitical priests. And it shall be with him, and he shall read it all the days of his life, that he may learn to fear the Lord his God, by carefully observing all the words of this law and these statutes."[2]

Since the Pentateuch and other writings that make up the Old Testament were considered holy, they were preserved with great care. There is adequate evidence from history that this preservation was consistent and precise.

The *Mishnah* (a codification of the traditional Jewish oral law, committed to writing around A.D. 200) supplies us with an unbroken historical tradition about the line of people responsible for the preservation of the text from the time of Moses until the Council of Jamnia (first century A.D.).

The sacred Torah-scrolls are kept in the Jewish synagogue in the "holy ark." The scrolls are reverently wrapped in cloth, often embroidered laborously with gold and silver threads. When such a book-scroll has become worn out, it is not thrown away but buried. A new scroll is, even today, transcribed by hand from the old, before the old is buried.

"Moses received the Law from Sinai and committed it to Joshua, and Joshua to the elders, and the elders to the Prophets, and the Prophets committed it to the men of the Great Synagogue. They said three things: be deliberate in judgment, gather up many disciples, and make a fence around the Law.

"Simeon the Just was of the remnants of the Great Synagogue. He used to say: by three things is the World sustained: by the Law, by the [temple] service, and by deeds of loving-kindness."[3]

The Council of Jamnia itself was very important. It solidified the Jewish canon of inspired books into the form we know as the Old Testament today. Biblical scholar F. F. Bruce commented:

"The books which they decided to acknowledge as canonical were already generally accepted, although questions had been raised about them. Those which they refused to admit had never been included. They did not expel from the canon any book which had previously been admitted. 'The Council of Jamnia,' as J. S. Wright puts it, 'was the confirming of public

43

opinion, not the forming of it.'"[4]

From the Mishnah and the tradition since the Council of Jamnia we have documented accounts of the history of the preservation of the Old Testament.

The Sopherim

From the completion of the Old Testament (400 B.C.) in the time of Ezra until the time of the Jewish scholars known as *Massoretes* (A.D. 500), the transmission and care of the Old Testament text was in the hands of a group of scribes. This group was called the *Sopherim* (meaning

The Samaritans are a mixed race of Israelites and Assyrian immigrants. They severed themselves completely from the Jews after the Babylonian Captivity. They recognize only the Pentateuch as divinely authoritative, having their own scrolls of it. Their text has not yet been ascertained officially. In spite of 1500 years of their separate transmission, their agreement with the text of the Massoretes is remarkable. Even today, there is still a small group possessing their own Torah, the Samaritan Pentateuch, which is sacred to them.

"counters"). The scribes got this name because of the manner in which they checked the accuracy of their copying of the texts. The Sopherim counted the number of letters in each completed copy and the number of words in each section of Scripture and compared them to the texts from which they copied. This minute accounting was described by biblical and literary scholar Sir Frederic Kenyon:

"Besides recording varieties of reading, tradition, or conjecture, the Massoretes undertook a number of calculations which do not enter into the ordinary sphere of textual criticism. They numbered the verses, words, and letters of every book. They calculated the middle word and middle letter of each. They enumerated verses which contained all the letters of the alphabet, or a certain number of them; and so on. These trivialities, as we may rightly consider them, had yet the effect of securing minute attention to the precise transmission of the text; and they are but an excessive manifestation of a respect for the sacred Scriptures which in itself deserves nothing but praise. The Massoretes were indeed anxious that not one jot nor tittle, not one smallest letter nor one tiny part of a letter, of the Law should pass away or be lost."[5]

The scribes went to great lengths to insure the purity of the materials used in the copies of the text and their own purity as transmitters of God's sacred Word. This was in addition to the great pains taken to insure the purity of the text itself, as we have seen above.

(1) A synagogue roll must be written on the skins of clean animals, (2) prepared for the particular use of the synagogue by a Jew. (3) These must be fastened together with strings taken from clean animals. (4) Every skin must contain a certain number of columns, equal throughout the entire codex. (5) The length of each column must not extend over less than 48 or more than 60 lines; and the breadth must consist of thirty letters. (6) The whole copy must be first-lined; and if three words be written without a line, it is worthless. (7) The ink should be black, neither red, green, nor any other colour, and be prepared according to a definite recipe. (8) An authentic copy must be the exemplar, from which the transcriber ought

not in the least deviate. (9) No word or letter, not even a yod, must be written from memory, the scribe not having looked at the codex before him... (10) between every consonant the space of a hair or thread must intervene; (11) between every new parashah, or section, the breath of nine consonants; (12) between every book, three lines. (13) The fifth book of Moses must terminate exactly with a line; but the rest need not do so. (14) Besides this, the copyist must sit in full Jewish dress, (15) wash his whole body, (16) not begin to write the name of God with a pen newly dipped in ink, (17) and should a king address him while writing that name he must take no notice of him.[6]

The Massoretes

The scribes called the Sopherim eventually became the preservers of the body of Jewish tradition. They were specialists in preserving the sacred writings, laws, history and tradition of the Jewish people. These specialists were known as the *Massoretes,* deriving their name from the Hebrew word *Massorah,* meaning "tradition." The Massoretes did their work in both Palestine and Babylon from approximately A.D. 500 to A.D. 900. They contributed to Old Testament textual preservation in several significant ways.

The Massoretes collected all the textual-critical remarks of the rabbis

The copyists of Bible books played a vital role in the transmission of Scripture texts. Letter by letter, word by word was transcribed. These scribes (Sopherim) had to keep to strict rules when they were copying. When the copy was done, all the letters and words were counted, and if even one was missing, the copying had to be done all over again. This strict control and the great reverence for the text have guaranteed the survival of the Bible through the ravages of time.

(Jewish teachers), all the additional marks added to the margins of the sacred texts (including memory devices, pronunciation aids, etc.), and entered these in the side margins of the copies they made. These marginal notes are known as the *Massorah Parva*. The Massoretes also did extensive tabulations concerning the contents of the texts and these were added to the upper and lower margins, with the overflow consigned to prefaces and appendices. These tabulations were known as the *Massorah Magna*.

The Massoretes considered the text so sacred that they never altered it even when the text they were copying contained an obvious copying error itself. Their procedure in such an instance was to enter the error into the text they were producing, with marginal remarks on how it could be corrected.

Another contribution of the Massoretes was their invention of a complete Hebrew vowel system as an aid in pronunciation. Hebrew is traditionally a language only of consonants, without vowels. Because the same combinations of Hebrew consonants could sound different with different vowel sounds, when Hebrew ceased to be predominately a spoken language, word pronunciation was forgotten. The Massoretes remedied this problem by inventing a system of symbols which were place above, midway, and underneath the consonants in the texts and yet did not interfere with the original consonant text at all. These "vowel points" are still used today in printed editions of the Hebrew Old Testament.

The Massoretes also added a system of accent indicators that aided in the public reading of the text and are still a great help in determining where a sentence or clause begins or ends.

The contributions of the Massoretes to the textual preservation of the Old Testament cannot be minimized. Not only did they carefully enhance understanding of the texts by their marginal contributions, they also carefully preserved all of the alternate readings of the texts, a service invaluable to today's textual critics in their work to determine the Old Testament's original text.

The establishment of a standard Hebrew text began in the latter half of the eighth century A.D. when a Jewish scholar, Moses Ben Asher, and his son, Aaron Ben Moses Ben Asher, put together what has become known as the Massoretic text. The Ben Naphtali family, contemporaries of the Ben Ashers, also established a specific Hebrew text. But it was the Ben Asher text that soon reigned as the commonly accepted and approved text of the Old Testament. That was due in part to the great Jewish philosopher Maimonides (1135-1204), who endorsed their work as follows: "All relied on it since it was corrected by Ben Asher and was worked on by him for many years and was proofread many times in accordance with the Massorah, and I based myself on this manuscript in the Sefer Torah that I wrote." Even so, the differences between the Ben Asher and Ben Naphtali texts are very minor consisting mostly of differences in spelling.

The Major Hebrew Manuscripts

The following is a list of the major Hebrew manuscripts we possess from the Massoretic tradition. These manuscripts are used by modern textual critics in reconstructing the original text of the Old Testament:

The Cairo Codex of the Prophets (designated as *C* for identification) contains the second division of the Hebrew Scriptures (see beginning of chapter) and was written around A.D. 895.

The Leningrad Manuscript Heb. B 3 (designated as *P* for Petrograd, former name of the Russian city of Leningrad) was composed in A.D. 916 and contains only the later prophets.

The Aleppo Manuscript (designated *A)* is from the tenth century. It has a scribal note stating that the vowels were added by Aaron Ben Asher (died A.D. 940). It contained the entire Old Testament when it was discovered, but about one fourth of it was later destroyed.

The British Museum OR. 4445 was probably written about the middle of the tenth century and contains only Genesis 39:20—Deuteronomy 1:33.

The Leningrad MS. B-19A (designated as *L)* was copied in A.D. 1008, from an earlier one prepared by Aaron Ben Moses Ben Asher and contains the entire Old Testament.

Why are there so few extant (existing) ancient copies of the Old Testament? The reason we do not possess many older copies of the Hewbrew Scriptures is because of the reverence with which the Jews protected the purity of God's Word. The Jews considered the text so sacred that they ceremoniously disposed of worn copies. The worn copies were first stored in a special room in the synagogue, called a *Genizah*. After a number of copies accumulated they were all buried together (usually in the grave of some Jewish scholar). The Jews believed that this would protect readers

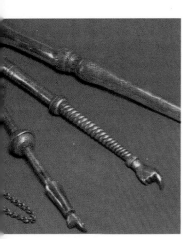

The text of the Bible is so sacred to the rabbis that it may not even be touched with a finger while they are reading it. For this reason delicate little hands of gold or silver are being used.

from misreading God's Word because of worn spots in older manuscripts. That practice accounts for our having very few early manuscripts of the Old Testament.

Accuracy was not lost by destroying the worn copies because of the meticulous care with which the Jews copied the manuscripts. The new copy was identical to the worn-out copy in every detail. Because the Jews considered the text so sacred, they refused to change it in any way. Editors and scribes, as we saw above, were reluctant to make changes even when it appeared obvious that the text from which they were copying had a copying error itself. Instead they would add a note referenced to the passage in question with their own suggestion for reconciliation of the problem, while still preserving the error in the main body of the text. First-century Jewish historian Flavius Josephus recorded this reverence for the Scriptures:

"We have given practical proof of our reverence for our own Scriptures. For, although such long ages have now passed, no one has ventured either to add, or to remove, or to alter a syllable; and it is an instinct with every Jew, from the day of his birth, to regard them as the decrees of God, to abide by them, and, if need be, cheerfully die for them. Time and again ere now the sight has been witnessed of prisoners enduring tortures and death in every form in the theatres, rather than utter a single word against the laws and the allied documents."[7]

Further Testimony to the Text of the Old Testament

In addition to the Hebrew manuscripts already mentioned, we possess further testimonies to the accuracy of our Old Testament text. Textual critics also consult the *Targums,* the Greek translations *(Septuagint),* the *Samaritan Pentateuch,* and the *Dead Sea Scrolls.* Let us now look at the evidence from each of these sources.

The Targums

The Targums were Jewish paraphrases of the Old Testament written mostly in the Aramaic language. The first recorded instance of a targum is found in the Old Testament itself. When Judah returned from its 70-year exile in Babylon, many of the people had forgotten Hebrew and now spoke Aramaic. That change made the Hebrew Scriptures incomprehensible to them. Those learned Jews who understood both languages read aloud to the citizens in Hebrew and them gave a paraphrase of the passage in Aramaic. This practice is recorded in Nehemiah 8:8 ("And they read from the book, from the Law of God, translating to give the sense so that they understood the reading").

That practice continued until the entire Old Testament, with the exception of the passages already in Aramaic in Daniel and Ezra, were given Aramaic paraphrases. The Targums, no matter how practical, were never given the holy authority accorded to the Hebrew originals. The Mishnah recorded the procedure by which the Old Testament with its Aramaic Targums was to be read to the people.

To textual critics, the Targums are helpful in establishing the correct text of the Old Testament. Some of the Targums date back centuries before the standard Massoretic text. The Palestinian Targum, for example, dates back to the time of Christ. The Targums had a long oral history before they were first recorded. They thus become a very ancient witness to the true text of the Old Testament.

The Septuagint

The Septuagint, the standard Greek translation of the Old Testament, was composed to meet the unique needs of the Greek-speaking Jewish community in Egypt during the Hellenistic period (about 250 B.C.). This large Jewish community was concentrated in the Egyptian city of Alexandria. The Jewish leaders in Alexandria began to translate the Old Testament into Greek around 250 B.C. The work of translation continued until after the time of Christ. The standardized Greek text of the whole Old Testament became known as the Septuagint (Greek for "seventy").

The Massoretes' most important task was to furnish the sacred text with vowels and punctuation signs. When Hebrew had vanished as a colloquial language, nobody knew precisely how the words had to be pronounced. The dots and strokes in the above text are the vowels and punctuation signs of the Massoretes. The pictured fragment is Manuscript 455, a page from Ecclesiastes.

The Septuagint is often abbreviated as LXX, the Roman numeral notation for *seventy*. According to tradition from around 100 B.C. (first recorded in a document known as the letter of Aristeas), the Septuagint was prepared by 70 learned Jews during a 70-day period, each working separately. The Lord so honored their effort, tradition goes, that when the scholars met, their translations were found to be identical to each other in every respect.

According to more reliable historical chronology, the Septuagint actually took several hundred years to complete. A variety of translators worked on the different books. Those translators exhibited a wide degree of competence, as biblical scholar H. B. Swete explains:

"The Pentateuch is on the whole a close and serviceable translation; the Psalms and more especially the Book of Isaiah show obvious signs of incompetence. The translator of Job was perhaps more familiar with Greek pagan literature than with Semitic poetry; the translator of Daniel indulges at times in a Midrashic [Jewish commentary or interpretation] paraphrase. The version of Judges which appears in our oldest Greek uncial MS. has been suspected by a recent critic of being the work of the 4th century A.D.; the Greek Ecclesiates savours of the school of Aquila."[8]

Because of the varying degrees of competence among translators, it is

49

difficult to tell if the translator was endeavoring to provide a word-for-word translation or an idiomatically equivalent translation. If the bulk of the LXX represents a literal (word-for-word) translation, then it offers differences from the later Massoretic text. The importance of the LXX is that it is an ancient witness to the text of the Old Testament. Even in those places where the text differs from the Massoretic text, the percentage of difference is not great and the differences do not represent significant changes in meaning. Some of the Greek manuscripts of the LXX that survive are from the fourth century A.D., hundreds of years before the Massoretic text was standardized. Moreover, since the translation was begun arouund 250 B.C., it is an important witness to the text

Besides dots and strokes for vowels and punctuation marks, the Massoretes also placed marginal notes next to the Hebrew text. These gave the reader editorial remarks, or proposed a variant reading for a certain word, whereas the consonantal text was never altered.

in use at the time of Christ.

Other Greek Versions

There were other Greek versions produced after the Septuagint. Aquila of Sinope, a Jewish convert *from* Christianity, made a slavishly literal translation of the Old Testament around A.D. 130 which many Pharisaical Jews used to replace the Septuagint. It survives today only in fragments.

Toward the end of the second century, Theodotian of Ephesus made a loose revision of the Septuagint from a massoretic type of Old Testament text. Only fragments of this work survive, but in our present text of the Septuagint, Theodotian's text has been preserved in Daniel and serves in place of the original Septuagint version of Daniel.

There were other miscellaneous Greek translations of the Old Testament, most of which are lost to us today. One was produced by Symmachus, a Jewish Ebionite. Others are known to us only by the Greek numbers Quinta, Sexta and Septima (five, six and seven). An important work was the Hexapla, composed by the early church writer, Origen (A.D. 185-254). This amazing work was an Old Testament harmony, providing the reader with Greek and Hebrew columns.

The Samaritan Pentateuch

Another source used by textual critics for the text of the Old Testament is the Samaritan Pentateuch. The people who lived in Samaria were a result of interbreeding of Jews and Assyrians. After the Babylonian captivity they cut themselves off entirely from the Jews (about 586 B.C.), and their development was independent from that point on. They possessed their own text of the Bible (only the Pentateuch), their own temple on Mt. Gerizim, and had their own cultural heritage. The New Testament gospel writer John reminds us that the Jews had no dealings with Samaritans (John 4:9).

The Samaritans believed that only the Pentateuch (first five books of the Old Testament) were the inspired word of God. They rejected both the Prophets and the Writings. The oldest manuscripts of the Samaritan Pentateuch still in existence date from the tenth century A.D. The Samaritan Pentateuch, written in a unique script with no vowel signs, differs little from the Massoretic text. Most of the differences are in spelling and grammar. What is truly remarkable is that their close similarity was maintained over a 1,500-year independence from each other. Textual criticism tells us, however, that the Massoretic text was more carefully preserved than the Samaritan Pentateuch.

The Dead Sea Scrolls

Until 1947 the oldest complete manuscript of the Old Testament in our possession dated from around A.D. 1000, a full 1,400 years after the completion of the Old Testament. Many speculated that during that long span of years significant changes could have crept into the text.

The Nash Papyrus was one of the oldest fragments of the Old Testament before the discovery of the Dead Sea Scrolls. This document, found in 1902 in Egypt by W. L. Nash, contains part of the Ten Commandments and of Deuteronomy 6:4ff. It dates from the 2nd or 1st century A.D.

In 1947, however, a dramatic event took place, which revolutionized textual criticism and laid to rest some of the best speculations against the veracity of the Old Testament text. In that year a young Bedouin goat herder was looking for a lost goat in the caves in the cliffs above Wadi Qumran, about a mile southwest of the northwest corner of the Dead Sea. In one cave he found several clay jars over two feet high and approximately ten inches wide. Those jars contained leather scrolls wrapped in linen cloth. Shortly after his find, some of the scrolls came into the hands of an antique dealer in Bethlehem; others were obtained by the archbishop of the Syrian Orthodox monastery in Jerusalem.

One of the first scholars to examine the scrolls was E. L. Sukenik, of the Hebrew University of Jerusalem, who immediately recognized their antiquity and value. The amazing find was confirmed by Dr. W. F. Albright, one of this century's eminent archaeologists. Confirming that the scrolls were of the Old Testament, Albright labeled the find "the most important Old Testament manuscript discovery ever made."

Recovery of more scrolls was halted by Arab-Israeli conflicts, so it was not possible to go back to investigate further until the peace of 1948. Investigation then revealed hundreds of scrolls in a dozen different caves. The scrolls had been placed there by a Jewish sect called the Essenes, who had established a fortress nearby which they occupied from about 100 B.C. to around A.D. 68, when they fled the advancing Roman armies. Before they abandoned their community they carefully hid their library in the nearby caves of Wadi Qumran. There they lay undisturbed for almost 1,900 years.

Analysis showed that the scrolls were composed mostly during those years between 100 B.C. and A.D. 68. The scrolls contain portions of every book of the Old Testament (except Esther) and numerous documents relating to the doctrines and practices of the Essenes. Particularly significant is the complete scroll of Isaiah, found in Cave 1 and dating to one hundred years before Christ. An important fragment of Samuel, dating 400 years before the birth of Christ, was found in Cave 4. These and other finds revolutionized Old Testament textual criticism.

The Dead Sea Scrolls provide abundant and clear evidence of the complete faithfulness of the Old Testament text to the originals in spite of transmission through long centuries. An example of that faithfulness can be seen by comparing the contemporary Hebrew text of Isaiah 53 with the same chapter in the Isaiah scroll from Qumran:

"Of the 166 words in Isaiah 53, there are only seventeen letters in question. Ten of these letters are simply a matter of spelling, which does not affect the sense. Four more letters are minor stylistic changes, such as conjunctions. The remaining three letters comprise the word 'light,' which is added in verse 11, and does not affect the meaning greatly.... Thus, in one chapter of 166 words, there is only one word (three letters) in question after a thousand years of transmission—and this word does not significantly change the meaning of the passage."[9]

After comparing the entire Isaiah manuscript from Qumran with the present Hebrew text of Isaiah, Old Testament scholar Gleason L. Archer concluded that the Dead Sea Scroll "proved to be word for word identical with our standard Hebrew Bible in more than 95 percent of the text. The 5 percent of variation consisted chiefly of obvious slips of the pen and variations in spelling."[10]

F. F. Bruce states that "the consonantal text of the Hebrew Bible which the Massoretes edited had been handed down to their time with conspicuous fidelity over a period of nearly a thousand years."[11]

Concerning the accuracy of the transmission of the Hebrew text, Atkinson, who was Under-Librarian of the library at Cambridge University, says it is "little short of miraculous."

There are fragments of the Greek translation of the Old Testament—the Septuagint (LXX)—which might even be older than existing Hebrew manuscripts. This Papyrus Rylands Greek 458 is from the middle of the second century B.C.

Other Ancient Writings

The books of the Old Testament were considered sacred by the Jews. However, other books were composed that were considered historically accurate and valuable. The Bible mentions some of these:

1.	The Book of the Wars of Jehovah	Num. 21:14
2.	The Book of Jasher	Joshua 10:13, 2 Sam. 1:18
3.	The Book of the Acts of Solomon	1 Kings 11:41
4.	The History of Nathan the Prophet	1 Chron. 29:29; 2 Chron. 9:29
5.	The History of Gad the Seer	1 Chron. 29:29
6.	The Prophecy of Ahijah the Shilonite	2 Chron. 9:29
7.	The Visions of Iddo the Seer	2 Chron. 9:29
8.	The History of Iddo the Seer	2 Chron. 12:15
9.	The Commentary of the Prophet Iddo	2 Chron. 13:22
10.	The History of Shemaiah the Prophet	2 Chron. 12:15
11.	The History (Book) of Jehu, son of Hanani	2 Chron. 20:34
12.	The History of Hozai	2 Chron. 33:19, R.V.
13.	The Commentary of the Book of the Kings	2 Chron. 24:27
14.	The Book of the Kings of Israel	1 Chron. 9:1; 2 Chron. 33:18
15.	The Book of the Chronicles of the Kings of Israel	1 Kings 14:19 *et. al*
16.	The Book of the Chronicles of the Kings of Judah	1 Kings 14:29 *et. al*

Evidently, most of these were official records housed in the royal archives. Although these works were considered authoritative, they were never placed on the same level as the writings that were considered Holy Scripture.

Summary and Conclusion

The evidence in support of the trustworthiness of the Old Testament text is overwhelming. It accurately represents the original. One of the great Old Testament scholars of our century, Robert Dick Wilson, affirmed that the preponderance of evidence is in favor of the veracity of the Old Testament text. He declared:

On the right: Not far from Herod's fortress, Masada (see picture), where the Jewish freedom fighters, the Zealots, resisted the Romans to the end after the fall of Jerusalem, lies Qumran. In 1947 the Dead Sea scrolls were found here. The Jewish sect of the Essenes had hurriedly left them behind when the Roman legions advanced.

Below: Some of these scrolls are now being shown to the public in a museum in Jerusalem, built specially for this purpose: The Shrine of the Book. The show-case (in the form of a "handle" of a book-scroll) contains, among others, the complete scroll of Isaiah that was found in Qumran.

"In 144 cases of transliteration from Egyptian, Assyrian, Babylonian and Moabite into Hebrew and in 40 cases of the opposite, or 184 in all, the evidence shows that for 2300 to 3900 years the text of the proper names in the Hebrew Bible has been transmitted with the most minute accuracy. That the original scribes should have written them with such close conformity to correct philological principles is a wonderful proof of their thorough care and scholarship; further, that the Hebrew text should have been transmitted by copyists through so many centuries is a phenomenon unequaled in the history of literature. . . . There are about forty of these [Old Testament] kings living from 2000 B.C. to 400 B.C. Each appears in chronological order. . . with reference to the kings of the same country and with respect to the kings of other countries. . . no stronger evidence for the substantial accuracy of the Old Testament records could possibly be imagined, than this collection of kings. Mathematically, it is one chance in 750,000,000,000,000,000,000,000 that this accuracy is mere circumstance. . . . The proof that the copies of the original documents have been handed down with substantial correctness for more than 2000 years cannot be denied. That the copies in existence 2000 years ago had been

In these and similar jars the Dead Sea Scrolls were found. Besides book-scrolls that have to do with the sect of the Essenes, fragments or whole scrolls of Bible books have been discovered. These Dead Sea Scrolls present irrefutable evidence of the accuracy of the Hebrew Bible text.

in like manner handed down from the originals is not merely possible, but, as we have shown, is rendered probable by the analogies of Babylonian documents now existing of which we have both originals and copies, thousands of years apart, and of scores of papyri which show when compared with our modern editions of the classics that only minor changes of the text have taken place in more than 2000 years and especially by the scientific and demonstrable accuracy with which the proper spelling of the names of kings and of the numerous foreign terms embedded in the Hebrew text has been transmitted to us."[12]

The oldest parts of the Old Testament are probably 3,400 years old, yet we can be confident that the text we possess today accurately represents what was originally written. Some of the indications of textual accuracy we have examined include:

1. When the manuscripts from the Massoretic tradition are compared among themselves, there are very few variant readings.

2. The Samaritan Pentateuch, the Targums and the Greek versions are in close harmony with the Massoretic text.

3. The reverence and care with which Jewish scribes throughout the centuries copied the text is a strong indication of the accuracy of the text.

4. The Dead Sea Scrolls give overwhelming confirmation that Hebrew texts separated by a thousand years agree in minute detail.

We can thus read the Old Testament with the assurance that we are reading what God originally delivered in the inspired (God-breathed) originals.

CHAPTER THREE

The Making of the New Testament

Page 56: The Monastery of St. Catherine in the heart of the Sinai Desert. Here Tischendorf found one of the most famous manuscripts of the New Testament: the Codex Sinaiticus.

On the right: The colonnade in Ephesus was already by Paul's time the main thoroughfare of the city. The road is 580 yards (530 meters) long and led from the city gate to the amphitheater on the mountain slope. In 391 the Roman emperor had declared Christianity to be the state religion here in Ephesus. But Ephesus had also been the center of the cult of Artemis (Diana), the goddess of human fertility, birth, youth and marriage. The apostle Paul was once the focal point of a tremendous uproar of the people of Ephesus, because of his zeal against the worship of the goddess Artemis (Acts 19:21-40).

The books of the New Testament were originally composed in *Koine* Greek, the most widely spoken language in the first century. As is true with the Old Testament, we do not possess the originals, or autographs, because of age. That makes us dependent on copies, and copies of copies to reconstruct the text. The question immediately arises, how good are the copies? How many of them exist? Can we be sure the text has not been significantly tampered with? As we saw with the Old Testament, we are going to see here that we can have complete trust in the text of the New Testament as being reliable.

The discipline that deals with the reconstructing of texts, whether or not they are biblical texts, is known as textual criticism. The reason for employing the science of textual criticism in New Testament study is twofold: (1) We do not possess the original manuscripts, and (2) the copies we possess differ in some areas. The textual critic, therefore, pieces together the evidence to reconstruct the original text. In the case of the New Testament three lines of evidence are available to reconstruct the original: the Greek manuscripts, the versions and the church fathers.

The Greek Manuscripts

How well have the *Koine* Greek manuscripts of the New Testament been transmitted?

57

The problem with almost all ancient writings is the lack of extant (existing) manuscripts to reconstruct the text. Most ancient writings have the most paltry manuscript evidence by which experts attempt to establish the original.

In the case of the New Testament, however, the problem disappears because we are not lacking manuscripts to reconstruct the text. On the contrary, we have an abundance of manuscripts, which makes the establishment of the text virtually certain.

In the history of the transmission of the Greek text we have found different lines of evidence: uncial manuscripts, minuscule manuscripts, lec-

The New Testament contains also a letter written by Paul to the church in Philippi, of which we see the ruins on this picture. The epistles of Paul form a substantial part of the New Testament and were mostly addressed to local churches. When a church had read the letter, it was often passed on to other churches so it could be read there, too (Colossians 4:16).

tionaries and the papyri.

Uncial writing, which consisted of upper-case letters (all capitals) that were deliberately and carefully written, is the type of writing used at the time of the composition of the New Testament. The uncial manuscripts were written between the fourth and tenth centuries. In the ninth century A.D., uncial writing began to be replaced with minuscule writing.

Minuscule writing was a script of smaller letters not as carefully executed as uncials; books could be turned out much faster by the employment of minuscule writing. Minuscule writing was in vogue from the ninth to the sixteenth centuries.

Regarding the third witness to the New Testament, lectionaries, Bruce Metzger explains:

"Lectionaries were the result of the Christian Church following the custom of synagogue. Every Sabbath different portions of the Law and Prophets were read at services. Likewise the Christians developed a similar practice, reading a different portion of the Gospels and Epistles according to a fixed order of Sundays and Holy Days. These Scripture lessons are known as Lectionaries."[1]

The earliest fragments of lectionaries come from the sixth century A.D. Complete manuscripts are found as early as the eighth century.

58

The last line of evidence of the Greek manuscripts is the papyri. Papyrus is the material which the original copies of the New Testament were composed. It is an extremely perishable material, surviving only in warm, dry climates. The papyrus fragments that have survived, however, contain some of the earliest witnesses to the New Testament text. The papyri were written with the uncial script.

The following chart lists some of the most important Greek manuscripts that have survived.

John Rylands Manuscript (designated papyrus 52, or p^{52}). This small fragment, located at the John Rylands Library in Manchester, England, is the oldest existing manuscript of the New Testament. The fragment containing John 18:31-33 on the front and John 18:37-38 on the back has been dated between A.D. 110 and 140.

Bodmer Papyrus. This collection of papyri manuscripts is found in the Bodmer Library, Geneva Switzerland. The most important of the Bodmer Papyri are:

p^{66}, which dates from about A.D. 150 and contains a large part of the Gospel of John, thus making it the oldest manuscript of the New Testament that contains anything extensive.

p^{72}, which dates from the third century and contains, among other things, 1 and 2 Peter and Jude.

p^{75}, which dates near the end of the second century and contains much of the gospels of Luke and John.

The Chester Beatty Papyri. the Chester Beatty Collection can be found variously in Dublin, Ireland, and the University of Michigan. It includes:

p^{45}, which dates from the early third century and contains about one seventh of the text of the gospels and Acts.

p^{46}, which dates from the early part of the third century and contains a large portion of Paul's epistles plus Hebrews.

p^{47}, which dates from the early part of the third century and contains a third of the book of Revelation.

Codex Sinaiticus (designated Aleph. א). This manuscript dating from the fourth century can be found in the British Museum. It was discovered in the last century by Constantine Tischendorf in the monastery of St. Catherine on Mt. Sinai (hence Sinaiticus). It contains both the complete Old and New Testament.

A (02) Codex Alexandrinus. This fifth-century manuscript can also be found in the British Museum. It contains most of both Testaments, lacking in the New Testament only most of Matthew and 2 Corinthians and part of the Gospel of John.

B (03) Codex Vaticanus. This fourth-century manuscript is located in the Vatican Library where it has resided for at least five centuries. It originally contained both Testaments but in the New Testament lacks part of Hebrews and all of Titus, Philemon, and Revelation.

C (04) Codex Ephraemi Rescriptus. This fifth-century manuscript, which contains almost all of the New Testament, resides in the Bibliotheque Nationale of Paris. It is a palimpsest, meaning that the original text was

The Codex Alexandrinus dates from the 4th century A.D. and contains the Old and the New Testaments. As a gift from the patriarch of Constantinople to king Charles I (1627) of England, the codex can now be seen at the British Museum in London. Since this codex became the property of the patriarch of Alexandria in 1078, it was named after this city.

scraped off and something was written over it. Through the use of chemicals, the erased portions of the text can be restored.

D (05) Codex Bezae. This sixth-century manuscript of the gospels and Acts is located in the Cambridge University Library. The text has many textual peculiarities, including a longer text of the Book of Acts.

D Paul (06) Codex Claromontanus. This sixth-century manuscript of the epistles of Paul and Hebrews resides in the Bibliotheque Nationale in Paris. Like Codex Bezae, it is a bilingual manuscript, having Greek and Latin on facing pages.

The Codex Bezae, from the 5th or 6th century A.D., presented by Calvin's student Beza to the University of Cambridge as a gift.

W (032) Codex Freericanus or Washingtonensis. This fourth-century manuscript is located at the Freer Art Gallery of the Smithsonian Institute in Washington, D.C.

We catalogue the surviving *Greek* manuscripts along the following lines: uncial manuscripts, minuscule manuscripts, lectionaries and papyri.

Type of Manuscript	Number Surviving
Uncial	267
Minuscule	2,764
Lectionaries	2,143
Papyri	88
Recent finds not catalogued	47
Total	5,309

The total number of surviving Greek manuscripts upon which the original New Testament text can be reconstructed dwarfs all other ancient works. Yet Greek manuscripts are not the only line of evidence available for this reconstruction.

Versions

Another line of evidence by which the New Testament text can be established, comes from the versions. Versions are translations of the different New Testament books into other languages. Although ancient literature was rarely translated into another language, the New Testament was an exception. From the beginning, Christian missionaries in an attempt to propagate their faith translated the New Testament into the various languages of the people they encountered. Some of those translations, made as early as the middle of the second century, give us an important witness to the text of that early time.

When the copies of the manuscripts of the versions are catalogued, we

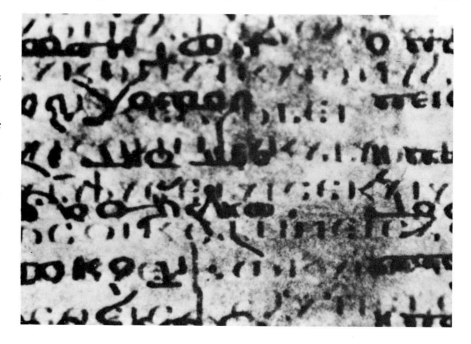

The Codex Ephraemi Rescriptus was the first important discovery by Tischendorf (pictured below). But many more were to follow. Three years after deciphering this document, Tischendorf, accompanied by four Bedouins, traveled into the desert on camel-back looking for ancient dry places, which had not yet been ransacked by Moslems. Chances were great that they would find very old manuscripts in those places.

are again faced with an overwhelming number. (It should be noted that when we speak of manuscripts or copies we are referring to any part of a manuscript or copy that has survived. Thus the copies could be anything from a mere fragment to a complete text.) The following breakdown illustrates this:

Versions	*Number of Manuscripts*
Latin Vulgate	10,000 +
	(may be as high as 25,000)
Ethiopic	2,000 +
Slavic	4,101 +
Armenian	2,587
Syriac Peshitta	350 +
Bohairic	100
Total	19,000 +

Since the versions are translations from the Greek, they are not as valuable as the Greek manuscripts in reconstructing the original text. They are, however, an important witness to the text's basic reliability.

Comparisons to Other Ancient Works

When the manuscript evidence for the New Testament text (Greek manuscripts and versions) is compared to other ancient writings the difference between them is striking — as the following chart reveals:

Work	Date Written	Earliest Copy	Time Span	Number of Copies
Euripides	480-406 B.C.	A.D. 1100	1,500 yrs.	9
Sophocles	496-406 B.C.	A.D. 1000	1,400 yrs.	193
Catullus	54 B.C.	A.D. 1550	1,600 yrs.	3
Aristophanes	450-385 B.C.	A.D. 900	1,200 yrs.	10
Homer *(Iliad)*	900 B.C.	400 B.C.	500 yrs.	643
New Testament	A.D. 40-100	A.D. 125	50 yrs.	Over 24,000

When reconstructing the text of an ancient work, a couple of questions need to be considered. The first question deals with the time span between the date the work was completed and the earliest existing copy. All other things being equal, the shorter the time span the more dependable the copy. The longer the time, the more errors are apt to creep in.

As we can see from the chart, the time span between the composition of the New Testament and the earliest existing copy is much shorter than for the other ancient works. Thus, using this standard of comparison, the New Testament comes out in even better shape.

Another question that needs to be asked concerns the number of copies. "How many copies are there to reconstruct the text?" The more copies you have, the better off you are — since there is then much more evidence to compare and help you to decide what the original said.

In the Monastery of St. Catherine in the Sinai Desert, on his first journey in 1844, Tischendorf found 43 pages of the Greek Old Testament in a waste-paper basket. In 1853 he again visited the monastery, but found nothing. Not until 1859, armed with a recommendation letter from the czar of Russia, did he find another 199 pages of the Greek Old Testament plus a complete Greek New Testament, The Codex Sinaiticus (A.D. 350).

For example, if an ancient work came down to us in only one copy, there would be nothing to compare that copy with. If the scribe was incompetent there is no way of knowing; you could not now check it against another copy. The more copies you have, the more comparisons can be made and the greater the chance of establishing the correct text. J. Harold Greenlee observes:

"The probability that the original text of a document has been preserved is in part dependent upon two factors concerning the manuscripts. In the first place, the shorter the interval of time between the original document and the date when the earliest available manuscript (or manuscripts) was written, the more likely it is that only a few copies intervene between this manuscript and the original and therefore the greater the probability that the text of this manuscript accurately reflects the text of the original. In the second place, the greater the number of available manuscripts, the greater is the probability that all of the original text has been preserved accurately among them."[2]

When the number of existing manuscripts of the New Testament is compared with other ancient writings, the New Testament completely overwhelms the others.

A comparison between Homer's *Iliad* and the New Testament will illustrate the superiority of the evidence for the Scripture. Bruce Metzger observes:

"Of all the literary compositions by the Greek people, the Homeric poems are the best suited for comparison with the Bible.". . . "In the entire range of ancient Greek and Latin literature, the *Iliad* ranks next to the New Testament in possessing the greatest amount of manuscript testimony.

"In antiquity men [1] memorized Homer as later they were to memorize the Scriptures. [2] Each was held in the highest esteem and quoted in defense of arguments pertaining to heaven, earth, and Hades. [3] Homer and the Bible served as primers from which different generations of school boys were taught to read. [4] Around both there grew up a mass of scholia and commentaries. [5] They were provided with glossaries. [6] Both fell into the hands of allegorists. [7] Both were imitated and supplemented — one with Homeric Hymns and writings such as the Batrachomyomachia, and the other with apocryphal books. [8] Homer was made available in prose analyses; the Gospel of John was turned into epic hexameters by Nonnus of Panopolis. [9] The manuscripts of both Homer and the Bible were illustrated. [10] Homeric scenes appeared in Pompeian murals; Christian basilicas were decorated with mosaics and frescoes of Biblical episodes."[3]

When comparing the two, the New Testament dwarfs the Iliad in manuscript evidence as the chart demonstrates. Moreover it must be remembered that, in manuscript authority, the Iliad is second to the New Testament of all the writings of antiquity!

The case for the primacy of the New Testament over other ancient writings in increased when further comparisons are made. F. F. Bruce comments: "Perhaps we can appreciate how wealthy the New Testament is in manuscript attestation if we compare the textual material for other ancient historical works. For Caesar's Gallic Wars (composed between 58 and 50 B.C.) there are several extant MSS, but only nine or ten are good, and the oldest is some 900 years later than Caesar's day. Of the 142 books of the Roman history of Livy (59 B.C. - A.D. 17), only 35 survive; these are known to us from not more than 20 MSS of any consequence, only one of which, and that containing fragments of Books III-VI, is as old as the fourth century. Of the 14 books of the Histories of Tacitus (ca

The Sinai Desert has very forbidding landscapes and was also one of the discovery sites of very old Bible manuscripts during the last century.

A.D. 100) only four and a half survive; of the 16 books of his Annals, 10 survive in full and two in part. The text of these extant portions of his two great historical works depends entirely on two MSS, one of the ninth century and one of the eleventh.

"The extant MSS of his minor works (Dialogus de Oratoribus, Agricola, Germania) all descend from a codex of the tenth century. The History of Thucydides (ca 460-400 B.C.) is known to us from eight MSS, the earliest belonging to ca A.D. 900, and a few papyrus scraps, belonging to about the beginning of the Christian era. The same is true of the History of Herodotus (B.C. 488-428). Yet no classical scholar would listen to an argument that the authenticity of Herodotus or Thucydides is in doubt because the earliest MSS of their works which are of any use to us are over 1,300 years later than the originals."[4]

Bruce Metzger writes of the comparisons:

"*The works of several ancient authors are preserved to us by the thinnest possible thread of transmission.* For example, the compendious history of Rome by Velleius Paterculus survived to modern times in only one incomplete manuscript, from which the *editio princeps* was made — and this lone manuscript was lost in the seventeenth century after being copied by Beatus Rhenanus at Amerbach. Even the *Annals* of the famous historian Tacitus is extant, so far as the first six books are concerned, in but a single manuscript, dating from the ninth century. In 1870 the only known manuscript of the *Epistle to Diognetus*, an early Christian compostion which editors usually include in the corpus of Apostolic Fathers, perished in a fire at the municipal library in Strasbourg. *In contrast with these figures, the textual critic of the New Testament is embarrassed by the wealth of his material.*"[5]

This being true, we have every right to believe that with such an abundance of manuscript evidence the text has come down to us without any loss. Yet when we have completed looking at the evidence from the Greek manuscripts and the versions we have still not exhausted the lines of evidence for reconstructing the New Testament text.

The Church Fathers

A third line of evidence can be consulted in establishing the New Testament text, quotations from the writings of men known as the "church fathers." In their writings the church fathers would often quote from the New Testament text. Every time we find a biblical quotation in their writings, we have another witness to the New Testament text.

For example, Ignatius (A.D. 70-110) wrote some seven letters in which he quoted from 18 different books of the New Testament. Every time he quotes a text, we can observe what Greek text he was using by his quotation. Thus, the early church fathers provide us with an excellent early witness to the text. One must use caution, however, in relying too heavily on the fathers; sometimes their quotations were paraphrases (not word for word). Also, the copies of the manuscripts of the writings of the fathers have gone through a period of copying, during which mistakes could have slipped into their text. Nevertheless, these *patristic* writings are an important witness to the original text.

The number of quotations of the fathers is overwhelming, so much so that, if every other source for the New Testament (Greek manuscripts, versions) were destroyed, the text could be reconstructed merely on the writings of the fathers. Consider the evidence:

"Sir David Dalrymple was wondering about the preponderance of Scripture in early writing when someone asked him. 'Suppose that the New Testament had been destroyed, and every copy of it lost by the end of the third century, could it have been collected together again from the writings of the Fathers of the second and third centuries?' After a great deal of investigation Dalrymple concluded: 'Look at those books. You remember the question about the New Testament and the Fathers? That question roused my curiosity and as I possessed all the existing works of the Fathers of the second and third centuries, I commenced to search and up to this time I have found the entire New Testament, except eleven verses.' "[6]

Leo Vaganay, writing of the patristic quotations of the New Testament, writes: "Of the considerable volumes of unpublished material that Dean Burgon left when he died, of special note is his index of New Testament citations by the church Fathers of antiquity. It consists of sixteen thick volumes to be found in the British Museum, and contains 86,489 quotations."[7]

Tischendorf was not the only one who made remarkable discoveries in the Monastery of St. Catherine. In 1978, the news media reported new findings of a very old text, discovered during reconstructions on the site. These texts are now being examined by the monks themselves.

Consequently, when the evidence from the Greek manuscripts, the versions and the church fathers is considered, any impartial person cannot help but be impressed. But two questions always come up when this issue is discussed. They concern the missing autographs (the originals) and the variant readings.

Missing Autographs

One question that always comes up when examining the issue of the New Testament text concerns the missing original manuscripts. Why didn't any of the originals survive? What are the reasons that we don't now possess

The Chester Beatty Papyri, a collection which contains parts of the New Testament, dates from the first half of the third century A.D.

the autographs of the New Testament books?

As has been said, one reason the originals are no longer with us is because of the material they were originally composed upon. Papyrus is extremely perishable. J. Harold Greenlee observes: "The autographs of the N. T. books were probably on papyrus and could hardly have survived except possibly in the dry sand of Egypt or in those conditions similar to those in the caves where the Dead Sea Scrolls have been found."[8]

There is also the possibility that the early scribe who copied the manuscripts observed the Jewish practice of destroying old worn-out copies when new ones were made. Kirsopp Lake comments: "It is hard to resist the conclusion that the scribes usually destroyed their exemplars when they copied the Sacred Books."[9]

One can also imagine other reasons they have not survived. It is highly likely that if the originals were still around they would become objects of veneration; the manuscript would be more important than the message. The tendency to venerate relics above what they stand for is always with us.

In the book of Numbers, God sent snakes into the camp of the complaining Israelites as a judgment against them. The people turned to Moses who then asked God for relief from the situation. God told Moses to erect a bronze snake on a pole in the center of the camp. Moses was to tell the Israelites that those who were bitten by the snakes could look to that bronze snake and live. The bronze snake had no power to heal, but it represented obedience to God. Centuries later, when going through the temple, that bronze snake was found. The people in turn began to worship the object. We may speculate that if the original manuscripts of the Scriptures were found, the same thing would happen.

Variant Readings

What is a variant reading? Simply stated, when two manuscripts differ

on a particular word or phrase in the text, the result is a variant reading. The difference may be of spelling, word order or different words employed. The variations in the text arose both unintentionally and intentionally.

Unintentional Variations

The greatest number of variants in the New Testament manuscripts are of the unintentional variety. They could creep into the text through faulty sight, hearing, writing, memory or judgment on the part of the scribe. Bruce Metzger writes:

"In the earliest days of the Christian church after an apostolic letter was sent to a congregation or an individual, or after a gospel was written to meet the needs of a particular reading public, copies would be made in order to extend its influence and to enable others to profit from it as well. It was inevitable that such handwritten copies would contain a greater or lesser number of differences in wording from the original. Most of the divergencies arose from quite accidental causes, such as mistaking a letter or a word for another that looked like it. If two neighboring lines of a manuscript began or ended with the same group of letters or if two similar words stood near each other in the same line, it was easy for the eye of the copyist to jump from the first group of letters to the second, and so for a portion of the text to be omitted (called homoeoercton or homoeoteleuton, depending upon whether the similarity of letters oc-

67

curred at the beginning or the ending of the words). Conversely the scribe might go back from the second to the first group and unwittingly copy one or more words twice (called dittography). Letters that were pronounced alike were sometimes confused (called itacism). Such accidental errors are almost unavoidable whenever lengthy passages are copied by hand, and would be especially likely to occur if the scribe had defective eyesight, or was interrupted while copying, or, because of fatigue, was less attentive to his task than he should have been."[10]

Intentional Variations

Some of the variations in the text came about intentionally. J. Harold Greenlee writes:

"These comprise a significant, although a much less numerous, group of errors than the unintentional changes. They derive for the most part from attempts by scribes to improve the text in various ways. Few indeed are the evidences that heretical or destructive variants have been deliberately introduced into the mss."[11]

Bruce Metzger expands upon the intentional variations:

"Other divergencies in wording arose from deliberate attempts to smooth out grammatical or stylistic harshness, or to eliminate real or imagined obscurities of meaning in the text. Sometimes a copyist would add what seemed to him to be a more appropriate word or form, perhaps derived from a parallel passage (called harmonization or assimilation). Thus, during the years immediately following the composition of the several documents that eventually were collected to form the New Testament, hundreds if not thousands of variant readings arose."[12]

At the head of the West German Institute for New Testament Textual Research in Münster stands Dr. Kurt Aland. His institute has already brought to light more than 1,200 previously unknown manuscripts. The Greek New Testament which was published here, the Novum Testamentum Graece, by Nestlé-Aland, has already been reprinted dozens of times.

It is often charged by those opposed to Christianity, that the variant readings in the manuscripts undermine the reliability of the text. These people point to some 200,000 variants in the existing manuscripts and contend that it is impossible to recover the New Testament's exact text and message. Nothing could be further from the truth.

It must be remembered that some 25,000 manuscripts of the New Testament exist in either Greek or one of the many versions. Every time one word or letter is different in a manuscript it is counted as a variant. For example, if a word is misspelled in 2,000 manuscripts it is counted as 2,000 variants: Most of the variants are of this variety and are only incidental to the meaning of the text. Here are some further examples:

In Luke 4:23, along with other places, there is a variation in the spelling of the name Capernaum. It is sometimes spelled Capharnaum. Every time this occurs it is counted as a variant.

In Mark 7:24 some manuscripts read "Tyre and Sidon." Others read "Tyre." Every time they differ it is counted as a variant.

In John 19:7 some manuscripts read "our law." Others read "the law." Every time they differ it is counted as a variant.

As stated, most of the variants do not materially affect the meaning of the text. At the turn of the century, B. B. Warfield observed that the New Testament "has been transmitted to us with no, or next to no, variation; and even in the most corrupt form in which it has ever appeared, to use the oft-quoted words of Richard Bentley, 'The real text of the sacred writers

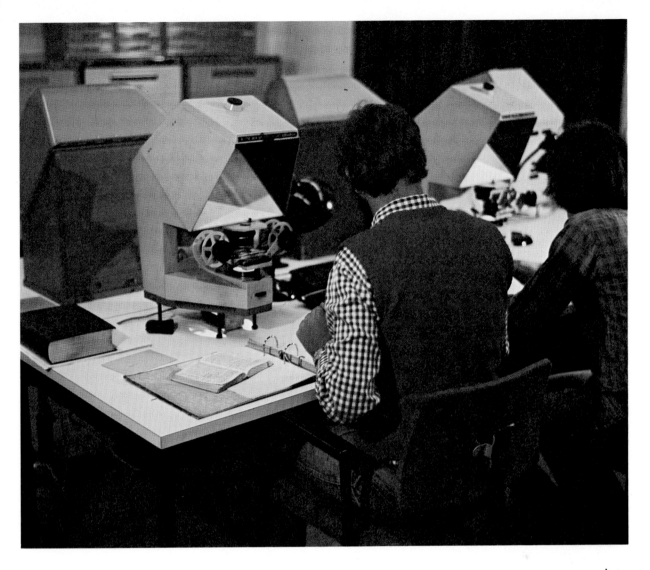

The institute in Munster keeps record of 95 per cent of all 5,400 manuscripts of the New Testament on micro-film. By carefully comparing the texts with each other, the original text can be established.

is competently exact.'"[13] Further, because we possess so many manuscripts, we can be assured of preserving the original text. The great scholar Samuel Tregelles stated, "We possess so many mss, and we are aided by so many versions, that we are never left to the need to conjecture as the means of removing errata."[14]

Summary and Conclusion

Although we do not possess the original manuscripts of any of the books of the New Testament, the evidence that it has been transcribed accurately through history is overwhelming. Consider the following:

1. The interval between the date of composition of the books and the earliest existing manuscripts is relatively short. Most other ancient works have a much longer gap between the time when they were composed and the earliest available manuscript (Caesar: 1,000 years, Herodotus: 1,600 years, etc.). The New Testament manuscripts go back to within 250 years of the time of composition, with some fragments going back even earlier. Since the classical writings are viewed as having been transcribed in a reliable manner, the New Testament documents, if considered on the same basis, also must be considered trustworthy.

2. Not only is the time interval shorter between the writings of the New

69

Testament and the earliest existing manuscripts, but the number of manuscripts (5,500 in Greek) is far superior to any other ancient work — where most are counted by the handful (Euripides: 9, Aristophanes: 10, Catullus: 3, etc.). Given the axiom, "The more manuscripts, the better chance to reconstruct the original," we again see that the New Testament has much more going for it than do other ancient works with regard to establishing the correct text.

3. The New Testament was translated into other languages at an early date. Those versions are another line of establishing the true text, and the number of manuscript copies of the different versions is around 20,000.

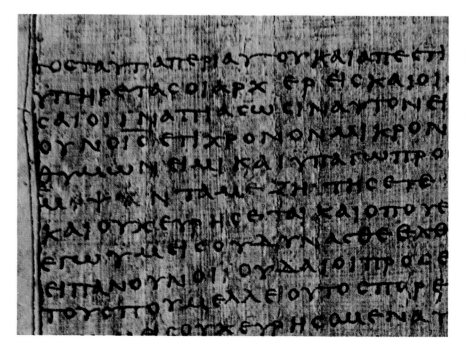

The Papyrus P⁶⁶ (published in 1956), the Bodmer Papyri, was named after M. Martin Bodmer, the founder of the Bodmer Library in Geneva, Switzerland. P⁶⁶ dates from around A.D. 200 and contains the Gospel of John. Since papyrus is such a perishable material (it was made from the stems of a kind of reed that grew along the Nile River), it was replaced by parchment in the 4th century A.D. This papyrus-codex originally contained about 75 sheets (thus 150 pages), of which two thirds came down to us in very good condition.

Other ancient writings have nothing in the way of evidence along this line, again making the New Testament stand out far and above other ancient works.

4. Still another line of evidence is found in the writings of the church fathers, where verses, passages and entire books are cited. There are enough references to be able to reconstruct the text totally apart from using any other line of evidence (Greek manuscripts or versions). Again, there is nothing anywhere like this for other ancient works.

Given these facts, we are forced to conclude that the New Testament has been transcribed accurately throughout history. Any contrary conclusion is based either on ignorance of the evidence or on a willful desire not to accept the facts as they stand. The late Sir Frederic Kenyon, keeper of ancient manuscripts and director of the British Museum, was an authority second to none. After a lifetime of study of ancient documents he came to the following conclusions:

"It cannot be too strongly asserted that in substance the text of the Bible is certain; especially is this the case with the New Testament. The number of manuscripts of the New Testament, of early translations from it, and of quotations from it in the oldest writers of the church, is so large that it is practically certain that the true reading of every doubtful passage is preserved in some one or other of these ancient authorities. This can be said of no other ancient book in the world."[15]

Kenyon also emphasized that:

"The interval then between the dates of original composition and the earliest extant evidence becomes so small as to be in fact negligible, and the last foundation for any doubt that the Scriptures have come down to us substantially as they were written has now been removed. Both the authenticity and the general integrity of the books of the New Testament may be regarded as finally established."[16]

Texts have not only been handed down to us on papyrus and on parchment, but old inscriptions on walls, pillars, coins and monuments, too, relate messages to us. This sarcophagus from the catacomb of Domitilla is a good, though fairly "young" example of this.

On the lower left, page 70: The potsherds (ostraca) from Lachish are much older. Between 1935 and 1940 archaeologists found 21 potsherds on this site, bearing military correspondence from the year 588 B.C. They reflect the critical situation of the last days of this city in Judah during the time of the siege before the Babylonian Captivity.

71

CHAPTER FOUR

The Canon and the Apocrypha

Above right: Another apocryphal book is the third addition to Daniel, containing the story of Susana. The picture shows this book in the dutch translation of the Statenbijbel, *where it has been included with a "caution to the readers."*

Now that we have determined that the texts of both the Old and New Testaments have been transmitted faithfully and accurately through the ages, we move on to the next logical step—the right of these documents to be considered part of the biblical canon, or list of approved books. How do we know we have the right books in our Bible? Are they adequate witnesses to the events they attempt to record? What about other books which claim (or have had claimed for them) the right to be considered Scripture, yet are missing from our common canon? This chapter concerning the canon (inspired collection) and apocrypha (separate writings) will deal with these and other questions.

The Canon

Scholars and clerics speak of the Old and New Testament books as belonging to the *canon of Scripture*. What is meant by that phrase? The word *canon* comes from the Hebrew word *ganeh* and the Greek word *kanon*. The word we have today carries with it the etymological idea of a reed or cane used as a measuring rod. The canon is thus the "measuring rod" or standard by which we judge a work's inspiration, authenticity and veracity.

73

Old Testament Books

We have already mentioned (in chapter two) that the Old Testament is divided into three sections: the Law, the Prophets and the Writings. We also showed that the (Protestant) church has the same books in its Old Testament as have the Jews throughout their history (although the Jewish order and numbering are different). We will now show that those books had been established as authentic and deserving of inclusion in the canon of Scripture long before the time of Jesus. They have every right to be considered the Word of God.

The fact that the Old Testament had a threefold division is recorded in the apocryphal book of Ecclesiasticus, written about 130 B.C. In its prologue, written by the author's grandson, the Old Testament is referred to as "...the Law, and the Prophets and the other books of the Fathers." That statement affirms the existence of the threefold division more than a hundred years before the time of Christ.

The Jewish historian Flavius Josephus also identified the canon of the Old Testament, saying,

> "For we have not an innumerable multitude of books among us disagreeing from the contradicting one another (as the Greeks have), but only twenty-two books, which contain the records of all the past times, which are justly believed to be divine. And of these, five belong to Moses, which contain his laws, and the tradition of mankind till his death. This interval of time was little short of three thousand years. But as to the time from the death of Moses till the reign of Artaxerxes, king of Persia, who reigned after Xerxes, the prophets, who were after Moses, wrote down what was done in their times in thirteen books. The remaining four books contain hymns to God, and precepts for the conduct of human life."[1]

Gleason Archer comments on the impact of this statement by Josephus:

> Note three important features of this statement: (1) Josephus includes the same three divisions of the Hebrew Scriptures as does the MT (although restricting the third group to "hymns" and *hokhmah*), and he limits the number of canonical books in these three divisions to twenty-two. (2) No more canonical writings have been composed since the reign of Artaxerxes, son of Xerxes (464-424 B.C.), that is, since the time of Malachi. (3) No additional material was ever included in the canonical twenty-two books during the centuries between (i.e., from 425 B.C. to A.D. 90). Rationalist higher critics emphatically deny the last two points, but they have to deal with the witness of such an early author as Josephus and explain how the knowledge of the allegedly post-Malachi date of sizable portions, such as Daniel, Ecclesiastes, Song of Solomon, and many of the psalms, had been kept from this learned Jew in the first century A.D. It is true that Josephus also alludes to apocryphal material (as from 1 Esdras and 1 Maccabees); but in view of the statement quoted above, it is plain that he was using it merely as a historical source, not as divinely inspired books.[2]

Josephus also declared:

> "...and how firmly we have given credit to those books of our own nation is evident by what we do; for during so many ages as have already passed, no one has been so bold as either to add anything to them or take anything from them, or to make any change in them; but it becomes natural to all Jews, immediately and from their very birth, to esteem those

The books of the Apocrypha, in contrast to the canonical books of the Bible, are not of divine authority. Nevertheless, they have been kept with love and handled with respect during the history of the Jews, preserved almost as carefully as these Torah-Scrolls which are in a synagogue in Cairo. The books of the Apocrypha were written in the time between the two Testaments, when different foreign powers occupied and ruled the land of Israel.

books to contain divine doctrines, and to persist in them, and, if occasion be, willingly to die for them. For it is no new thing for our captives, many of them in number, and frequently in time, to be seen to endure racks and deaths of all kinds upon the theatres, that they may not be obliged to say one word against our laws, and the records that contain them."[3]

A further witness to the Old Testament canon is given in various places in the Talmud:

Tosefta Yadaim 3:5 says: "The Gospel and the books of the heretics do not make the hands unclean; the books of Ben Sira and whatever books

One of the foreign rulers over Israel was Alexander the Great (356-323 B.C.), who, like a whirlwind, overran the whole of the Middle-East, from Egypt to India. That meant the end of the Persian Empire and the beginning of Greek dominion.

have been written since his time are not canonical."

Seder Olam Rabba 30 writes: "Up to this point [the time of Alexander the Great] the prophets prophesied through the Holy Spirit; from this time onward incline thine ear and listen to the sayings of the wise."

Babylonian Talmud, Tractate "Sanhedrin" VII-VIII, 24 declares: "After the latter prophets Haggai, Zechariah, and Malachi, the Holy Spirit departed from Israel."

Jesus Christ himself testified to the canon of the Old Testament. While Jesus never disagreed with the writings we find in our Old Testament today, He did, however, disagree with some of the oral traditions handed down by the religious rulers in Israel. Jesus Christ accepted the books of the Old Testament in the same threefold division that was common to the Jews of His day:

Now He said to them, "These are My words which I spoke to you while I was still with you, that all things which are written about Me in the Law of Moses and the Prophets and the Psalms must be fulfilled."[4]

Jesus Christ also testified to the extent of the Old Testament canon. In Luke 11:51 he spoke of "...the blood of Abel to the blood of Zechariah." Abel was the first martyr in Scripture (Genesis 4:8) and Zechariah was the last martyr named in the Jewish arrangement of the Old Testament (where 2 Chronicles is listed as the last book of the Old Testament: 2 Chronicles 24:21). Jesus thus gave His approval to the entire canon of the Old Testament with the same contents we have today.

Old Testament Apocrypha

Comments made previously in our book, *Answers to Tough Questions,* concerning the Old Testament apocryphal books are appropriate here:

"Today the word apocrypha is synonymous with the 14 or 15 books of doubtful authenticity and authority. These writings are not found in the Hebrew Old Testament, but they are contained in some manuscripts of

One important reason certain books of the New Testament were canonical is the fact that the writers thereof were disciples, eyewitnesses of the miracles Jesus performed, like the healing of the blind man.

the Septuagint, the Greek translation of the Hebrew Old Testament, which was completed around 250 B.C. in Alexandria, Egypt.

Most of these books were declared to be Scripture by the Roman Catholic Church at the Council of Trent (1545-1563), though the Protestant Church rejects any divine authority attached to them.

Those who attribute divine authority to these books and advocate them as Scripture argue that the writers of the New Testament quote mostly from the Septuagint, which contains the apocrypha. They also cite the fact that some of the church fathers, notably Irenaeus, Tertullian and Clement of Alexandria, used the apocrypha in public worship and accepted it as Scripture, as did the Syriac Church in the fourth century.

St. Augustine, who presided over the councils at Hippo and Carthage, concurred with their decision that the books of the apocrypha were inspired. The Greek Church adds its weight to the list of believers in the inspiration of apocrypha.

The advocates point also to the Dead Sea Scrolls to add further weight to their belief in the apocrypha. Among the fragments at Qumran are copies of some of the apocryphal books written in Hebrew. These have been discovered alongside the Old Testament works.

The case for including the apocrypha as holy Scripture completely breaks

76

down when examined. The New Testament writers may allude to the apocrypha, but they *never* quote from it as holy Scripture or give the slightest hint that any of the books are inspired. If the Septuagint in the first century contained these books, which is by no means a proven fact, Jesus and His disciples completely ignored them.

Appealing to certain church fathers as proof of the inspiration of the books is a weak argument, since just as many in the early church, notably Origen, Jerome and others, denied their alleged inspiration.

The Syriac Church waited until the fourth century A.D. to accept these books as canonical. It is notable that the Peshitta, the Syriac Bible of the second century A.D., did not contain them.

The early Augustine did acknowledge the apocrypha, at least in part. But later, Augustine's writings clearly reflected a rejection of these books as outside the canon and inferior to the Hebrew Scriptures.

The Jewish community also rejected these writings. At the Jewish Council of Jamnia (c. A.D. 90), nine of the books of our Old Testament canon were debated for differing reasons whether they were to be included. Eventually they ruled that only the Hebrew Old Testament books of our present canon were canonical.

Citing the presence of the apocrypha among the Old Testament fragments proves little regarding inspiration, as numerous fragments of other, non-Scriptural documents were also found.

It cannot be overemphasized that the Roman Catholic church itself did not officially declare these books Holy Scripture until 1545-1563 at the Council of Trent.

The acceptance of certain books in the apocrypha as canonical by the Roman Catholic church was to a great extent a reaction to the Protestant Reformation. By canonizing these books, they legitimized their reference to them in doctrinal matters.

The arguments that advocate the scriptural authority of the apocrypha obviously leave a great deal to be desired.

There are some other telling reasons why the apocrypha is rejected by the Protestant church. One of these deals with the unbiblical teaching of these questionable books, such as praying for the dead.

Praying for the deceased, advocated in II Maccabees 12:45-46, is in direct opposition to Luke 16:25, 26 and Hebrews 9:27, among others. The apocrypha also contains the episode which has God assisting Judith in a lie (Judith 9:10, 13).

The apocrypha contains demonstrable errors as well. Tobit was supposedly alive when Jeroboam staged his revolt in 931 B.C. and was still living at the time of the Assyrian captivity (722 B.C.), yet the Book of Tobit says he lived only 158 years (Tobit 1:3-5, 14:11).

Finally, there is no claim in any of these apocryphal books as to divine inspiration. One need only read these works alongside the Bible to see the vast difference."[5]

The New Testament was not written just by the apostles belonging to the "Twelve." Paul (painted the 18th century by the French artist L. G. Blanchet, Museum Calvet in Avignon) also wrote, as well as James, the brother of Jesus, and Mark and Luke, closest co-laborers of the apostles, and others.

The Dead Sea Scrolls

The Dead Sea Scrolls contribute to our knowledge of the canon.

The canon is the collection of Biblical books received as genuine and inspired. The Jewish synagogue and the Protestant church have the same

77

canon of the Old Testament. The Roman Catholic church accepts the 39 books of this canon as inspired, but it also accepts the collection of books which are known as apocrypha as part of the Catholic Bible.

We would like to know what books were deemed canonical by the Qumran community. A simple answer cannot be given because of the very nature of ancient writing materials. Each book existed as a single scroll. There is no bound collection of writings—such as our Bible—of which one could say, "These are our sacred books." the leaders of the Qumran community could have told us which of the scrolls were considered inspired Scripture, but no list of such writings has come down to us. In some sense

all of the documents kept in the library were considered authoritative—even the commentaries—but as Jews faithful to the tradition of the fathers there was doubtless a special regard for the Law (or Torah). Creeds, confessions of faith, and other writings are considered binding by Christian communities which consider the Bible as the word of God in a unique sense.

Indicative of the fact that the Old Testament as we have it was regarded as sacred Scripture at Qumran is the fact that every book except Esther is represented, at least in the form of fragments. In editing the Zadokite work, Chaim Rabin notes that quotations or allusions to every book in the Old Testament except Joshua, Joel, Jonah, Haggai, Ruth, and Lamentations are made in that document. since the Zadokite work is related to the Qumran community, and copies of it have been found at Qumran, this gives added testimony to the canon of Scripture. Thus every book of the Old Testament is found either in manuscript, quotation or allusion in the Qumran literature. The absence of Esther from the Qumran library may be due to the fact that it was not composed among Palestinian Jews. Since its locale is Persia it may not have been well known by the Qumranians. It is not quoted in the New Testament.

While apocryphal literature is found in abundance among the Qumran documents it is worthy of note that all of the commentaries thus far identified are of canonical books. In addition to the Cave 1 Habakkuk Commentary, fragments have been found of commentaries on Genesis 49, Psalms 37, 45, 57, 68; Isaiah (one in Cave 3 and another in Cave 4), Hosea, Micah, Nahum and Zephaniah. It would appear that only the canonical books were considered important enough to warrant interpretative commentaries.[6]

New Testament Books: Primary Source Testimony

As we investigate the New Testament text we are struck by the fact that the writers of the New Testament books claimed to be either eyewitnesses of the events recorded or those who gathered eyewitness testimony concerning them.

"What was from the beginning, what we have heard, what we have seen with our eyes, what we beheld and our hands handled, concerning the Word of Life — and the life was manifested, and we have seen and bear witness and proclaim to you the eternal life, which was with the Father and was manifested to us — what we have seen and heard we proclaim to you also, that you also may have fellowship with us; and indeed our fellowship is with the Father, and with His Son Jesus Christ."[7]

"Inasmuch as many have undertaken to compile an account of the things accomplished among us, just as those who from the beginning were eyewitnesses and servants of the Word have handed them down to us, it seemed fitting for me as well, having investigated everything carefully from the beginning, to write it out for you in consecutive order, most excellent Theophilus; so that you might know the exact truth about the things you have been taught."[8]

"For we did not follow cleverly devised tales when we made known to you the power and coming of our Lord Jesus Christ, but we were eyewitnesses of His majesty."[9]

"Now I make known to you, brethren, the gospel which I preached to you, which also you received, in which also you stand, by which also you are saved, if you hold fast the word which I preached to you, unless you believed in vain. For I delivered to you as of first importance what I also received, that Christ died for our sins according to the Scriptures, and that He was buried, and that He was raised on the third day according to the Scriptures..."[10]

The fact that the New Testament writers claimed such objective, complete, and firsthand evidence concerning Jesus Christ is of crucial importance in helping to determine the New Testament canon. Their evidence is not hearsay or imaginary: it is direct and reliable. Biblical scholar F. F. Bruce observes:

"The earliest preachers of the gospel knew the value of...first-hand testimony, and appealed to it time and again. 'We are witnesses of these things,' was their constant and confident assertion. And it can have been by no means so easy as some writers seem to think to invent words and deeds of Jesus in those early years, when so many of His disciples were about, who could remember what had and had not happened.

"And it was not only friendly eyewitnesses that the early preachers had to reckon with; there were others less well disposed who were also conversant with the main facts of the ministry and death of Jesus. The disciples could not afford to risk inaccuracies (not to speak of willful manipulation of the facts), which would at once be exposed by those who would be only too glad to do so. On the contrary, one of the strong points in the original apostolic preaching is the confident appeal to the knowledge of the hearers; they not only said, 'We are witnesses of these things,' but also, 'As you yourselves also know' (Acts 2:22). Had there been any tendency to depart from the facts in any material respect, the possible presence of hostile witnesses in the audience would have served as a further corrective."[11]

One of the earliest testimonies concerning the New Testament canon was made by the early church father, Irenaeus:

A chalk-drawing of the apocryphal story of Susanna. Further additions to the book of Daniel are the story of Bel and the Dragon and the Song of the Three Hebrew Children in the Furnace.

"Matthew published his Gospel among the Hebrews [i.e., Jews] in their own tongue, when Peter and Paul were preaching the gospel in Rome and founding the church there. After their departure [i.e., death, which strong tradition places at the time of the Neronian persecution in 64], Mark, the disciple and interpreter of Peter, himself handed down to us in writing the substance of Peter's preaching. Luke, the follower of Paul, set down in a book the gospel preached by his teacher. Then John, the disciple of the Lord, who also leaned on His breast [this is a reference to John 13:25 and 21:20], himself produced his Gospel, while he was living at Ephesus in Asia."

Irenaeus also confirmed that even the heretics could not deny the New Testament canon:

"So firm is the ground upon which these Gospels rest, that the very heretics themselves bear witness to them, and, starting from these [documents], each one of them endeavours to establish his own particular doctrine."

Irenaeus even recognized and considered as commonly accepted that there were four gospels in the inspired canon:

"For as there are four quarters of the world in which we live, and four universal winds, and as the Church is dispersed over all the earth, and the gospel is the pillar and base of the Church and the breath of life, so it is natural that it should have four pillars, breathing immortality from

80

every quarter and kindling the life of men anew. Whence it is manifest that the Word, the architect of all things, who sits upon the cherubim and holds all things together, having been manifested to men, has given us the gospel in fourfold form, but held together by one Spirit."

Dating of the New Testament

When all of the historical and textual evidence is amassed, it becomes clear that the New Testament was composed at a very early date by eyewitnesses and/or by those who recorded eyewitness testimony. Eminent archaeologist William F. Albright concluded:

"In my opinion, every book of the New Testament was written by a baptized Jew between the forties and the eighties of the first century A.D. (very probably sometime between A.D. 50 and 75)."[12]

Albright also reported:

"Thanks to the Qumran discoveries, the New Testament proves to be in fact what it was formerly believed to be: the teaching of Christ and his immediate followers between cir. 24 and cir. 80 A.D."[13]

Other Writings

Now that we have determined that the 27 books contained in the New Testament give a reliable and firsthand account of the events in the life of Jesus Christ and the early church, we focus on other writings that have not been placed in the New Testament canon but for which some individuals have claimed divine inspiration.

Close examination shows that these books, accepted by some people as canonical, lack the necessary integrity to be included in the New Testament canon. These books include:

The letter of Pseudo-Barnabas—supposedly composed around A.D. 75 and similar in style to the book of Hebrews. Its content is mystical and allegorical. It is an ancient document, but its authenticity is unverifiable.

The Shepherd of Hermas—the New Testament apocryphal work closest to being a canonical book. Even so, its composition as late as A.D. 125 eliminates it.

The Didache—the "teaching of the twelve," composed around A.D. 110. It gives the opinions of those living in the early part of the second century as to the basic doctrines of Christianity. Because of its content and late composition, it is not acceptable as a part of the New Testament canon.

Some of the other books occasionally considered inspired include The Letter to the Corinthians (A.D. 95-100); The Second Letter of Clement (A.D. 130); The Apocalypse of Peter (A.D. 150); and The Acts of Paul and Thecla (A.D. 170). Although these writings are of historical interest they are not of the spiritual, historical, or inspirational caliber of the canonical books. They do not contain eyewitness testimony.

Some books, rejected by all, are outright forgeries. These are called "pseudepigrapha." They were produced by heretics and cultists seeking to validate their heresies with pseudo-apostolic and Christological blessing. Authors Norman Geisler and William Nix give a summary of the most important of these forgeries:

Besides the canonical gospels of Matthew, Mark, Luke and John, there are also other gospels, like the Gospel of Thomas, pictured below. Brill, in Leyden (Netherlands), published an official edition in 1959 of the Coptic text together with the Dutch, English, German and French translations.

81

1. **The Gospel of Thomas** (first century), a Gnostic view of Jesus' childhood miracles.

2. **The Gospel of the Ebionites** (second century), Gnostic Christians maintained Old Testament practices in this work.

3. **The Gospel of Peter** (second century), a Docetic and Gnostic forgery.

4. **Protevangelium of James** (second century), a story from Mary to the massacre of babies.

5. **The Gospel of Egyptians** (second century) ascetic teaching against marriage, meat and wine.

6. **Arabic Gospel of Childhood** (?), childhood miracles in Egypt. Zoroastrian magi.

7. **The Gospel of Nicodemus** (second or fifth century), contains *Acts of Pilate* and *Descent of Jesus.*

8. **The Gospel of Joseph the Carpenter** (fourth century), the writing of the Monophysite cult that glorified Joseph.

9. **The History of Joseph the Carpenter,** (fifth century), Monophysite version of the life of Joseph.

10. **The Passing of Mary** (fourth century), bodily assumption and advanced stage of Mary worship.

11. **The Gospel of Nativity of Mary** (sixth century), promotes Mary worship and is the basis of the Golden Legend, a thirteenth century best seller on the lives of the saints by James or Orogeny.

12. **The Gospel of Pseudo-Matthew** (fifth century), visit to Egypt and later boyhood miracles of Jesus.

13-21. **The Gospel of the Twelve; The Gospel of Barnabas; The Gospel of Bartholomew; The Gospel According to the Hebrews; The Gospel of Marcion; The Gospel of Andrew; The Gospel of Matthias; The Gospel of Peter; The Gospel of Philip,** etc.

Athanasius (here pictured on a mosaic in St. Marks Cathedral in Venice) published a list of canonical books in A.D. 367.

"...Although the canons, councils and orthodox Fathers never considered the Pseudepigrapha to be inspired, because of their exaggerated fancy and heretical tendencies, they no doubt reflect fragments of truths behind their excesses, and they do reveal the consciousness (and corruption) of sections of the church even in the early centuries."[14]

After examining the evidence for the inclusion of our New Testament books in the canon and the evidence against including the apocryphal and pseudepigrapha in the canon, we can safely conclude that the New Testament we have today is the complete complement of books God wants us to include.

Biblical scholar J. I. Packer summarizes why we hold to the present canon of Scripture:

"A question, however, remains. If we may not ascribe infallibility to the Church's discernment of which books were to be inspired (and how can we?), then how may we be sure that our New Testament does not contain either too many books or too few? How can we be confident about the limits of the New Testament when we are so poorly placed, nearly two

The book of Ecclesiastes is one of the "antilegomena," i.e., its place within the canon was disputed by some. This probably was caused by the fact that it portrays a skeptical view of life. The preacher describes life "under the sun"; and beautiful as a sunset might be (as this one by Crete), he coldnot find any fulfilment in that kind of a life, until he learned to see things from God's point of view.

thousand years on, to check the early Church's verdicts about the authorship and authenticity of each item in it? The answer is found by stringing together the following facts.

"1. Christianity had both the idea and the reality of canonical Scripture from the start: for Christianity began as a Jewish sect, and Judaism was based on revering what we call the Old Testament as God's *torah* (law, instruction). Jesus confirmed this attitude to His disciples by letting them see that in these Scriptures He recognized His Father's voice, and that under their authority He lived and taught and died, not breaking them but fulfilling them. Naturally, therefore, pioneer missionaries like Paul gave the Old Testament to Gentile churches, which otherwise would not have known it, to function alongside apostolic teaching as their rule of faith and life. 'All Scripture is inspired by God and profitable...that *the man of God*' — the Christian! and in this instance, the minister — 'may be complete, equipped for every good work' (2 Tim. 3:16, R.S.V.). All of it was written 'for *our* learning, that...through comfort of the Scriptures *we*' — we Christians! — 'might have hope' (Rom. 15:4; cf. 1 Cor. 10:11). It is basic to Christianity to receive the Old Testament as Christian Scripture.

"2. An expectation of new canonical Scripture to stand beside the Old

Testament is implicit in the work of God on which Christianity rests. New and climactic revelation came via Jesus to the apostles for the world, and it would have been incomprehensible if the God who caused His earlier revelation to be recorded for posterity had not done the same for that which completed and fulfilled it. When Jesus prayed for the whole Church, apart from the apostles, as those who should 'believe on Me through their word' (Jn. 17:20), He assumed permanent availability of that word, which looks very much like anticipating an apostolic New Testament.

"3. A New Testament (as it was called from the second century) actually emerged, as a collection of more or less occasional writings which all assume authority as authentic communication of God's once-for-all revelation in Christ, and whose authors all identify themselves either by name or by relationship (thus, the author of Hebrews, anonymous to us, is a well-known colleague of Timothy [Hebrews 13:23]). Theories of pseudonymous authorship of New Testament books (what was once called forgery) have been dilligently explored over many years; here I can only say that none known to me convinces me, and I see strong external grounds in every case for concluding that each book is by the person whose name it bears, quite apart from the evidence of its own internal quality.

For some time, 2 Peter, too, was disputed. But it is evident from the Bodmer Papyrus P ⁷² that the letter was highly valued by the Coptic Christians in the third century. Clement of Rome had quoted from this letter of Peter already in the first century. Leonardo da Vinci made this drawing of Peter, which is now located in the Albertina in Vienna, Austria.

"4. A number of spurious books ascribed to apostolic authors exist for comparison with our New Testament, and the drop in intellectual, moral, and spiritual calibre is very marked, as are the theological lapses into worlds of commonplace fantasy and magic. In the light of this comparison, there is no reason to think that anything inauthentic crept into the New Testament, or that anything available by a genuine apostolic writer was negligently left out.

"5. The Church corporately testifies that the New Testament evidences itself to be the Word of God in a way that no other literature save the Old Testament does. As Jewish guards said of Jesus, 'Never man so spake' (Jn. 7:46), so God's people down the generations say of the New Testament, 'Never did writing make such an impact on heart and mind and conscience, communicating God, giving knowledge of oneself before God, mediating fellowship with Christ and renewing disordered lives.' Thus has the New Testament evidenced itself through the Spirit to be the Word of God; thus it does still.

"The action of making us aware of the divine quality of biblical books, the divinity which is the source of the power and authority with which we find them addressing us, is the so-called 'inner witness of the Holy Spirit' in relation to Scripture. This 'inner witness' is not a particular experience or feeling, nor is it a private revelation; it is another name for that enlightenment of our sinful hearts whereby we come to recognize and receive divine realities for what they are — Jesus Christ as our divine Saviour, Lord and Friend, and Holy Scripture as God's Word to us."[15]

Summary and Conclusion

After reviewing the evidence for the New Testament canon as we have it today, we come to certain conclusions:

1. The books that are in both the Old and New Testaments deserve their places as part of the divine revelation from God to humankind. They give firsthand testimony to the events they record. This is confirmed internally as well as by history.

2. Other books, such as the apocrypha, cannot meet the test of canonicity. Their exclusion from the canon is justified.

After the death of Alexander the Great, his Greek Empire was divided into four parts. Palestine finally came under the reign of the Seleucids, who also ruled over Syria. One of them - pictured on the coin - was Antiochus Epiphanes (the Mighty), but he soon received the nickname "Epimanes" (the Maniac). He committed cruelties and sacrilege like none other. The reaction of the Jews can be seen in the revolt of the family of the Maccabees. The most famous son of Mattathias, Judas Maccahaeus, inspired Handel to compose an oratorium, while Gustav Doré pictured him in this victorious pose. The Maccabees finally succeeded in driving out the Seleucids. These events are described in the apocryphal books of the Maccabees.

Our next step in exploring God's Word will be to examine the important question of inspiration. Are these books of the Old and New Testaments really the inspired, inerrant Word of God? The next two chapters will explore that issue.

CHAPTER FIVE

The Bible and Inspiration

Page 86: "In Him (the Incarnate Word) was life; and the life was the light of men. And the light shines in the darkness; and the darkness did not comprehend it" (John 1:4,5).

Above right: When Jesus Christ, the Word of God incarnate, walked on this earth, the light broke through the darkness. Even death had to flee. The raising of Lazarus from the dead was an eloquent witness to this fact.

Our journey through the Bible now brings us to a discussion of the inspiration and authority of Scripture. We have seen already that the books of the Bible have been transmitted accurately and are reliable witnesses to the events they portray. Now two questions will be addressed: Are the books of the Bible more than reliable historical literature? Are the books of the Bible the Word of God?

The Nature of Inspiration: Four Perspectives

One can view the Bible and its inspiration from several different perspectives. We will take a brief look at four of those perspectives before we produce a workable definition of the nature of biblical inspiration.

1. The Bible is an inspiring book but no different from other great literary works of the past.

This view places the Scriptures on the same level as other human productions. It categorically denies the possibility of God's providing a revelation of Himself through the books of the Bible.

2. The Bible is "in part" the Word of God.

This view limits the manner and quantity in which a revelation of God can be contained in the books of the Bible. Proponents of this view say,

"The Bible contains the Word of God," or "The Bible becomes the Word of God."

The idea that the Bible *contains* the Word of God makes the individual reader the final determiner of inspiration. How is one to determine which parts of the Bible are part of God's revelation and which parts are of only human origin? When the individual, or even a community of individuals (as in a church), becomes the determiner of inspiration, he or they become entangled in their own system. They have no adequate way of discerning whether the inspiration is inherent in certain parts of Scripture (and thus recognizable in some way by them), or perhaps they determine what is inspired, making biblical inspiration subjective rather than inherent. Such an inspiration is not only not taught in the Bible, but is virtually useless in clearly ascertaining God's revelation to humankind.

The idea that the Bible somehow contains the Word of God is an inadequate view of inspiration and is not biblically based. This view teaches that the Scriptures have no authority apart from the working of the Holy Spirit who at times mystically "energizes" portions of them. This approach to inspiration effectively shifts the authority of God's revelation from the Scriptures to the interpreter. Herman Ridderbos explains:

"No matter how much truth it may contain, this view [of inspiration] is beset with danger. For by identifying the Word of God with the present operation of the Spirit in the preaching, there is the ever present risk that first the Word of God itself, and then the canon may be completely identified with what the church understands or thinks it understands. The situation may even develop so far that God's word coincides with what the individual person experiences when the Scriptures are preached. In this way the door is thrown wide open to a subjectivistic and existentialistic view of God's word and of the canon."[1]

3. The Bible is the divine Word of God dictated by God to selected human authors.

This view leaves no room for the personal diversities of the various individual writers, diversities clearly evident in the Bible. Although it is popular among liberals and nonreligious persons to accuse all serious or conservative Christians (evangelicals) of holding this position, it is actually not a tenable position. James I. Packer notes:

"Because Evangelicals hold that the biblical writers were completely controlled by the Holy Spirit, it is often supposed...that they maintain what is called the 'dictation' or 'typewriter' theory of inspiration.... But it is not so. This 'dictation theory' is a man of straw. It is safe to say that no Protestant theologian, from the Reformation till now, has ever held it; and certainly modern Evangelicals do not hold it.... It is true that many sixteenth and seventeenth-century theologians spoke of Scripture as 'dictated by the Holy Ghost.' But all they meant was that the authors wrote word for word what God intended.... The use of the term 'dictation' was always figurative.... The proof of this lies in the fact that, when these theologians addressed themselves to the question, What was the Spirit's mode of operating in the writers' minds? they all gave their answer in terms not of dictation, but of accommodation, and rightly maintained that God completely adapted His inspiring activity to the cast of mind, outlook, temperament, interests, literary habits, and stylistic idiosyncrasies of each writer."[2]

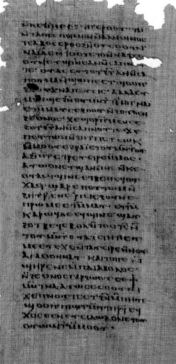

In 1945/46, 13 codices were discovered in Nag Hammadi, Southern Egypt. One of them is Codex VI, 33: The Revelation of Adam to Seth (Coptic Museum, Old Cairo). It is one of the many Old Testament forgeries dating from between 200 B.C. and A.D. 200.

4. The Bible is a book that is both divine and human.

In expanded form, this view reflects the biblical teaching that the Bible itself, in all that it states, is a product of divine revelation, channeled through, but not corrupted by, human agency, by which the unique talents, backgrounds and perspectives of the authors complement rather than restrict what God intended to reveal.

"All Scripture is inspired by God and profitable for teaching, for reproof, for correction, for training in righteousness."[3]

"But know this first of all, that no prophecy of Scripture is a matter of one's own interpretation, for no prophecy was ever made by an act of

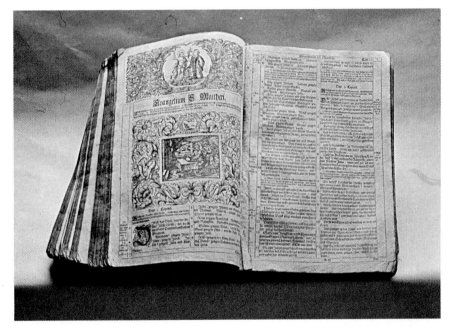

Pictured is an edition of Luther's Bible which strongly furthered the cause of the Reformation in German speaking areas.

human will, but men moved by the Holy Spirit spoke from God."[4]

Our English word *inspired* comes from a Greek term *(theopneustos)*, meaning "God-breathed." The source of all Scripture is God. The Scriptures, while inspired by God, are also the product of being channeled through men. These men recorded divine truth as they were led by the Holy Spirit. A great theologian, B. B. Warfield, put it this way:

"The Church, then, has held from the beginning that the Bible is the Word of God in such a sense that its words, though written by men and bearing indelibly impressed upon them the marks of their human origin, were written, nevertheless, under such an influence of the Holy Ghost as to be also the words of God, the adequate expression of His mind and will. It has always been recognized that this conception of co-authorship implies that the Spirit's superintendence extends to the choice of the words by the human authors (verbal inspiration), and preserves its product from everything inconsistent with a divine authorship—thus securing, among other things, that entire truthfulness which is everywhere supposed in and asserted for Scripture by the biblical writers (inerrancy). Whatever minor variations may now and again have entered into the mode of statement, this has always been the core of the Church doctrine of inspiration."[5]

Authors Norman Geisler and William Nix give an excellent working definition of inspiration in their General Introduction to the Bible:

"Inspiration is that mysterious process by which the divine causality worked through the human prophets without destroying their individual personalities and styles, to produce divinely authoritative writing."[6]

It is important to understand that this claim of inspiration is made by the Scriptures themselves. It is not something imposed on them by the church. From Genesis through Revelation the writers of Scriptures believed they were recording the Word of God. Consistently we find phrases like "Thus saith the Lord,"; "God said," "The Word of the Lord came unto...," and so on.

The words that the Holy Spirit gave to them were a holy trust, unviolated by their participation in the transmission. The apostle Paul declared, "and for this reason we also constantly thank God that when you received from us the word of God's message, you accepted it not as the word of men, but for what it really is, the word of God, which also performs its work in you who believe" (1 Thessalonians 2:13).

Extent of Inspiration

We shall repeat our citation of 2 Timothy 3:16 in preface to our discussion of the extent of inspiration:

"All Scripture is inspired by God and profitable for teaching, for reproof, for correction, for training in righteousness."

Two important principles can be drawn from this passage. Inspiration of Scripture is plenary, meaning that it includes the entire body of Scripture. It is also verbal, meaning that it includes the very words chosen.

Plenary Inspiration

"All" Scripture—the entire corpus of Scripture—is inspired by God. Inspiration is plenary, or "full." Every portion is "God-breathed." Some verses alluding to this are Revelation 22:18, 19; Matthew 5:17, 18; Romans 15:4; Jeremiah 15:19; 26:2; 36:2; and Luke 24:44, which is reproduced here:

"Now He said to them 'These are My words which I spoke to you while I was still with you, that all things which are written about Me in the Law of Moses, the Prophets and the Psalms must be fulfilled.'"

The clear teaching of Scripture is that the whole of it is inspired by God. Everything is considered accurate. That does not mean, however, that every statement in the Bible itself teaches truth. Satan's words, for example, are recorded accurately and are there because God wanted them there. But Satan did not tell the truth (John 8:44).

Verbal Inspiration

The Scripture indicates that inspiration extends not only to all of Scripture as a whole but to every word. It is not merely the thoughts or intentions of Scripture that are divinely inspired. Some of the verses upholding verbal inspiration include Jeremiah 1:7, 9; Exodus 34:27; John 6:63; and Matthew 4:4, where Jesus says,

"It is written 'Man shall not live on bread alone, but on every word that proceeds out of the mouth of God.'"

The truth of this teaching can be found in the fact that the apostles sometimes based their arguments on just one word of Scripture. For example, the apostle Paul cited a prophecy from the Old Testament and argued on the basis of one word in the Old Testament passage: "Now

The risen Savior appears to Mary Magdalene.

After His resurrection from the grave He commanded His followers to be His witnesses even to the remotest part of the earth (Acts 1:1-11).

the promises were spoken to Abraham and to his seed. He does not say, 'And to seeds,' as referring to many, but rather to one, 'And to your seed,' that is, Christ"[7]

The apostle John recorded an assertion by Jesus Christ in which He appropriated for Himself a divine title of God recorded in just one place in the Old Testament. The Jews, who had a high view of verbal inspiration, understood exactly what he meant. Rejecting His divine claim, they sought to stone Him for blasphemy: "Jesus said to them, 'Truly, truly, I say to you, before Abraham was born, *I AM.*' [the reference is to Exodus 3:14] Therefore they picked up stones to throw at Him; but Jesus hid Himself, and went out of the temple."[8]

"The wind blows where it wishes and you hear the sound of it, but do not know where it comes from and where it is going; so is every one who is born of the Spirit" (John 3,8).

Fallible Men Versus Infallible Bible

An obvious question arises. How could fallible men produce an infallible Bible?

One of the most frequent arguments leveled against the infallibility of the Bible is based upon the fact that the Bible was written by human authors. Human beings are fallible. Since the Bible was written by these fallible human beings, it necessarily follows that the Bible is fallible. Or so the argument goes. As Roman Catholic theologian Bruce Vawter writes, "A human literature containing no error would indeed be a contradiction in terms, since nothing is more human than to err."[9]

Although we often hear this accusation, it just is not correct. We grant that human beings do make mistakes, and that they make them often. But they do not necessarily make mistakes in all cases, and they do not necessarily have to make mistakes.

For example, several years ago one of the authors was teaching a class on the reliability of the Bible. For it, he had typed up a one-page outline of the course. The finished product was inerrant; it had no typographical errors, no mistakes in copying from the handwritten original. Although the author was human and was prone to make mistakes, he was in fact

91

infallible in this instance.

The point is this: It is not impossible for a human being to perform a mistake-free act. It is not impossible for fallible man to correctly record both sayings and events. Thus to rule out the possibility of an inerrant Bible by appealing to the fallibility of men does not hold up.

John Warwick Montgomery, lawyer/theologian, illustrates this truth: "The directions for operating my washing machine, for example, are literally infallible; if I do just what they say, the machine will respond. Euclid's Geometry is a book of perfect internal consistency; grant the axioms and the proofs follow inexorably. From such examples (and they could readily be multiplied) we must conclude that human beings, though they often err, need not err in all particular instances.

"To be sure, the production over centuries of sixty-six inerrant and mutually consistent books by different authors is a tall order — and we cheerfully appeal to God's Spirit to achieve it — but the point remains that there is nothing metaphysically inhuman or against human nature in such a possibility. If there were, have we considered the implications for christology? The incarnate Christ, as a real man, would also have had to err; and we have already seen that error in His teachings would totally negate the revelational value of the incarnation, leaving man as much in the dark as to the meaning of life and salvation as if no incarnation had occurred at all."[10]

We also believe that there is sufficient evidence that the Bible is the infallible Word of God. The Scriptures themselves testify, "All Scripture is God-breathed" (2 Timothy 3:16). If they contain error then one must call it God-inspired error. This is totally incompatible with the nature of God as revealed in the Bible. For example, Titus 1:2 says God cannot lie. John 17:17 says, "Thy word is truth."

Examples could be multiplied. The testimony of Scripture is clear. God used fallible men to receive and record His infallible Word so that it would reach us, correct and without error. Sounds difficult? With our God it's not. As He said (Jeremiah 32:27, NASB), "Behold I am the Lord, the God of all flesh; is anything too difficult for Me?"

What About Contradictions?

If the Bible is the divinely inspired Word of God, then God is the one who is eventually responsible for its content. This being the case, we need to address the matter of so-called contradictions that are contained within its pages. A Bible containing errors or contradictions is inconsistent with the God which it reveals. We will observe that a close evaluation of the matter shows that the Bible does not disagree with itself.

One of the things for which we appeal with regard to possible contradictions is fairness. We should not minimize or exaggerate the problem, and we must always begin by giving the author the benefit of the doubt. This is the rule in other literature, and we ask that it also be the rule here. We find so often that people want to employ a different set of rules when it comes to examining the Bible, and to this we immediately object.

What constitutes a contradiction? The law of non-contradiction, which is the basis of all logical thinking, states that a thing cannot be both *a* and *non-a* at the same time. In other words, it cannot be both raining and not raining at the same time.

If one can demonstrate a violation of this principle from Scripture, then and only then can he prove a contradiction. For example, if the Bible said—which it does not—that Jesus died by crucifixion both at Jerusalem and at Nazareth at the same time, this would be a provable error.

When facing possible contradictions, it is of the highest importance to remember that two statements may differ from each other without being contradictory. Some fail to make a distinction between contradiction and difference.

For example, the case of the blind men at Jericho. Matthew relates how two blind men met Jesus, while both Mark and Luke mention only one.

However, neither of these statements denies the other, but rather they are complementary.

Suppose you were talking to the mayor of your city and the chief of police at city hall. Later, you see your friend, Jim, and tell him you talked to the mayor today. An hour later, you see your friend, John, and tell him you talked to both the mayor and the chief of police.

When your friends compare notes, there is a seeming contradiction. But there is no contradiction. If you had told Jim that you talked *only* to the mayor, you would have contradicted that statement by what you told John.

The statements you actually made to Jim and John are different, but not contradictory. Likewise, many biblical statements fall into this category. Many think they find errors in passages that they have not correctly read.

In the Book of Judges we have the account of the death of Sisera. Judges 5:25-27 is supposed to represent Jael as having slain him with her hammer and tent peg while he was drinking milk. Judges 4:21 says she did it while he was asleep. However, a closer reading of Judges 5:25-27 will reveal that it is not stated that he was drinking milk at the moment of impact. Thus, the discrepancy disappears.

Sometimes two passages appear to be contradictory because the translation is not as accurate as it could be. A knowledge of the original languages of the Bible can immediately solve these difficulties, for both Greek and Hebrew—as all languages—have their peculiarities that make them difficult to render into English or any other language.

A classic example concerns the accounts of Paul's conversion as recorded in the Book of Acts. Acts 9:7 (KJV) states, "The men which journeyed with him stood speechless, hearing a voice, but seeing no man." Acts 22:9 (KJV) reads, "And they that were with me saw indeed the light, and were afraid; but they heard not the voice of Him that spake to me."

These statements seem contradictory, with one saying that Paul's companions heard a voice, while the other account says that no voice was heard. However, a knowledge of Greek solves this difficulty. As the Greek scholar, W.F. Arndt, explained:

One of the jars in which the Dead Sea Scrolls were found (Louvre, Paris).

"The construction of the verb 'to hear' (*akouo*) is not the same in both accounts. In Acts 9:7 it is used with the genitive, in Acts 22:9 with the accusative. The construction with the genitive simply expresses that something is being heard or that certain sounds reach the ear; nothing is indicated as to whether a person understands what he hears or not.

"The construction with the accusative, however, describes a hearing which includes mental apprehension of the message spoken. From this it becomes evident that the two passages are not contradictory.

"Acts 22:9 does not deny that the associates of Paul heard certain sounds; it simply declares that they did not hear in such a way as to understand what was being said. Our English idiom in this case simply is not so expressive as the Greek."

It must also be stressed that when a possible explanation is given to a Bible difficulty, it is unreasonable to state that the passage contains a demonstrable error. Some difficulties in Scripture result from our inadequate knowledge about the circumstances, and do not necessarily involve an error. These only prove that we are ignorant of the background.

As historical and archaeological study proceed, new light is being shed on difficult portions of Scripture and many "errors" have disappeared with the new understanding. We need a wait-and-see attitude on some problems.

While all Bible difficulties and discrepancies have not yet been cleared up, it is our firm conviction that as more knowledge is gained of the Bible's past, these problems will fade away. The biblical conception of God is an all-knowing, all-powerful being who does not contradict Himself, and so we feel that His Word, when properly understood, will not contradict itself.

The Authority of Jesus Christ

When it comes to determining whether or not the Bible is the inspired Word of God we can rest confidently on the authority of Jesus Christ. We arrive at this conclusion by the following logic:

1. We have already shown that the New Testament can be trusted as an accurate historical document, giving firsthand information on the life of Jesus Christ.

2. In this accurate, historical document Jesus Christ is presented as having made certain claims about Himself. He claimed to be the Messiah,

the Son of God, the Way, the Truth, and the Life, the only way by which anyone can approach God.

3. Jesus Christ demonstrated that He had the right to make those Old Testament claims by fulfilling prophecies about the Messiah. He performed miracles, showing He had power over nature. The most significant miracle of all was His rising from the dead (John 2:19-21). The resurrection confirmed His claims to deity.

4. Since Jesus is the Messiah, God in human flesh, He is the last word on all matters. He had the divine authority to endorse all Scripture or some. He universally affirmed all Scripture, in every part, as the divine Word of God.

The apostle John, here pictured in a valuable antique icon, is the Apostle of Love (John 13:23 and 21:20) who wrote about the Son of God's love. He is the one into whose care Jesus committed His mother Mary (John 19:26,27). With his own eyes he saw the empty grave and believed (John 20:8), and, finally, he is the one who in the last book of the Bible—the Revelation of Jesus Christ to John—is allowed to see the Resurrected One in His coming glory (Revelation 1:9-20).

The crucial issue of the inspiration of the Old Testament is solved by Jesus Christ and His attitude toward it. We see Jesus viewing the Old Testament with total trust, considering it the Word of God. See Matthew 15:3, 6; 22:31, 32; John 10:35; and Matthew 5:18.

If Jesus is who He claimed to be, God in human flesh, then His view of Scripture is of paramount importance. We see Him constantly referring to it as sacred in His teachings and in discussions with the religious leaders of His day. See Matthew 19:4; Luke 20:17; John 10:34; and Matthew 12:3.

He also quoted Scripture as divinely authoritative in His dialogues with Satan during His temptation. See Matthew 4:4, 7, 10.

If He said that the Old Testament is God's Word in every portion, then we can trust that. We see Him confirming the historicity of the Old Testament. See Matthew 19:1-4; 12:39-41; 24:15; Luke 4:17-21; and Matthew 13:14). So it is clear that Jesus Christ considered the Old Testament to be the authoritative Word of God. He constantly referred to it, authenticating some of its most controversial parts. The conclusion is clear: since

Jesus is God and authenticates the whole body and every portion of the Old Testament, we can conclude that it is the inspired Word of God.

Summary and Conclusions

1. The claim of inspiration is something the Bible makes for itself. It is not something that pious Christian believers have imposed on it. The clear teaching of Scripture is that it is the inspired Word of God.

2. The word inspiration literally means "God-breathed."

3. The Bible's inspiration is plenary, meaning that all parts of it are inspired by God. The Bible does not say that it "contains" the Word of God; it *is* the Word of God.

4. The Bible's inspiration is verbal, meaning that it extends to each and every word.

5. Though written by fallible men, the Bible was superintended by the Holy Spirit to produce an error-free book.

6. The Scripture does not disagree or contradict itself. The so-called contradictions of Scripture can be explained by a further examination of the evidence.

7. The inspiration of Scripture is confirmed by observing Jesus Christ's attitude toward it. Jesus Christ believed and taught that every word of the whole body of Scripture is the revealed Word of God.

"For just as Jonah was three days and three nights in the belly of the sea-monster; so shall the Son of Man be three days and three nights in the heart of the earth" (Matthew 12:40). The Bible speaks with absolute authority in matters of salvation as well as history, the universe and nature. The pictured miniature is taken from a medieval breviary (Bibliothéque Nationale, Paris).

CHAPTER SIX

The Historical Reliability of the Old Testament

The question of whether the Bible is historically accurate in its description of persons, places, and events is of crucial importance. If the message of the Bible is to be taken seriously, then the recording of historical events must be accurate. We cannot trust the theological observations of writers who cannot observe and report historical events correctly.

Biblical scholar F. F. Bruce echoes these thoughts:

"That Christianity has its roots in history is emphasized in the Church's earliest creeds, which fix the supreme revelation of God at a particular point in time, when 'Jesus Christ, His only Son our Lord...suffered under Pontius Pilate.' This historical 'once-for-all-ness' of Christianity, which distinguishes it from those religious and philosophical systems which are not specially related to any particular time, makes the reliability of the writings which purport to record this revelation a question of first-rate importance."[1]

In this chapter we will discover that historical events recorded in the Old Testament are accurate insofar as it is possible to determine them from present external evidence. (There are some events described in the Bible for which there is as yet no external historical evidence. Obviously that cannot be seen as a mark against the historical reliability of the Old Testament.)

Although the chronology of the history of the ancient Middle East in connection with Israel is an issue that is hotly debated by archaeologists, historians and others, there is no consensus of opinion in these matters, and we will review several possible chronologies in our third volume. But whatever view you follow or consider, one thing is clear: The historical facts which the Bible mentions are totally reliable and the model must be started by taking into account these facts rather than criticizing them from some outside position. The examples given in this chapter will confirm the accuracy of the Bible in the more or less generally accepted chronology.

ARCHAEOLOGY AND OLD TESTAMENT TIMES

Approx. Date	Palestine/Syria/Jordan	Also Called	Assyria/Babylonia	Egypt
B.C.		*I. Prehistoric*		
-8000	Paleolithic	(Old) Stone Age		
8000-6000	Mesolithic	Middle Stone Age		
		Natufian		
		Tahunian/Jerichoan		
6000-4000	Neolithic	Prepottery N.	Ubaid	Prehistoric
		Pottery N. (5000-)		
4000-3200	Chalcolithic	Ghassulian (end)	Uruk	Tasian
3200-3000	Esdraelon		Proto-Literate	Badarian
				Naquada I-II
		II. Bronze Age		
3000-2800	Early Bronze (Age) I	Early Canaanite	Early Dynastic	Pre-Dynastic I
	(= EB)	(= EC)	(= ED) I	
2800-2600	EB II		ED II	Archaic Period
				Dyn. I-III
2600-2300	EB III		ED III	Old Kingdom
				Dyn. III-IV
2300-2200	EB IV	EB IIIb	Sargonid	Dyn. V-VI
2200-1950	Intermediate	EB-MB	Ur III	First Intermediate
	Bronze (= IB)	MB I/MCI		Period
1950-1750	Middle Bronze	Middle Canaanite	Early Old Babylonian	Dyn. VII-XI
	(= MB) I	(= MC) IIa		Middle Kingdom (XII)
1750-1600	MB IIa	MB/MC IIb	Late Old Babylonian	Second Intermediate
				Dyn. XII-XVII
1600-1550	MB IIb	MB/MC IIc	Kassite	
1550-1400	Late Bronze	Late Canaanite	Middle Assyrian	New Kingdom (XVIII-)
	(= LB)	(= LC)	Middle Babylonian	
1400-1300	LB IIa	LC IIa		
1300-1200	LB IIc	LC IIc		Dyn. XIX
		III. Iron Age		
1200-1150	Iron (Age) Ia	(Early) Israelite		
	(= I)	Early Iron (= EI) I		
1150-1025	Ib			Dyn. XX Late Period
1025-950	Ic	EI II	Neo-Assyrian	Dyn. XXI
950-900	Id			Dyn. XXII (Libyan)
900-800	IIa	Middle Iron		
		Middle Israelite (= MI) I		
		Israelite II (970-840)		
800-700	IIb			Dyn XXIII-XXV
700-600	IIc	MI II		Dyn. XXVI (Saite)
		Israelite III (840-580)		
600-330	III	Late Iron	Neo-Babylonian	Dyn. XXVII-
		Late Israelite(= LI)	(Chaldean)	
		Israelite IV		
		Persian		
		IV. Hellenistic Age		
330-165	Hellenistic I		Hellenistic	Hellenistic Egypt
				Dyn. XXVIII-XXX
165-63	Hellenistic II	Hellenistic-Herodian		
		Maccabean		
63-A.D.70	Hellenistic-Roman			Roman

We must emphasize that we do not believe that the Bible is the Word of God merely because it records history accurately. Correct historical reporting does not determine inspiration. One cannot have credible inspiration, however, with faulty historical records.

Old Testament History

The Old Testament records events that span thousands of years. That time span can be divided into various periods. The chart on page 100 gives a useful categorization of the Old Testament time period.

Biblical scholar John Bright correctly points out the Bible's own high view of history:

A manuscript, showing a part of the Pentateuch (Leviticus 5:18-6:5), from the beginning of the 10th century A.D., provided with marginal notes by the Massoretes.

"The genius of the Old Testament faith does not lie in its idea of God or in the elevation of its ethical teachings. Rather, it lies in its understanding of history, specifically of Israel's history, as the theatre of God's purposive activity. The Old Testament offers a theological interpretation of history. A concern with the meaning of history, and of specific events within history, is one of its most characteristic features. It records a real history, and it interprets every detail of that history in the light of Yahweh's sovereign purpose and righteous will. It relates past events—the stories of the Patriarchs, the Exodus, the covenant at Sinai, the giving of the Promised Land—in terms of his gracious dealings with his people, his promise to them and its fulfillment. It continually sets forth the response that Yahweh requires of his people, and interprets their fortunes in the midst of events, in terms of their obedience or disobedience to his demands. And it announces that Yahweh will yet do, in the judgment of Exile and beyond, for the accomplishment of his purpose. The Old Testament consistently views Israel's history as one that is guided on to a destination by the word and will of her God."[3]

R. K. Harrison, noted Old Testament scholar and historian, emphasized the important role of archaeology in affirming the historical reliability of the Old Testament:

101

"...archaeology must not be regarded as the sole determining consideration in matters of historical criticism, since it, too, is beset with its own kind of problems. These include poor excavating techniques in earlier days, the varied interpretation of specific artifacts, and the difficulty of establishing an assured chronological framework into which events can be placed with confidence. Archaeology is in no sense an adequate "control" mechanism by which OT historic sequences stand or fall.

"Nevertheless, archaeological discoveries have assisted enormously in demonstrating the historicity of certain OT events and personages, and in other areas have furnished an authentic social and cultural background against which many OT narratives can be set with assurance. Numerous cuneiform texts that have been unearthed show how the Mesopotamian writers of early historiographic material expressed themselves in terms of a world view, as is the case in the first few chapters of Genesis, thereby indicating that the latter should not be taken as myth, but as Mesopotamian historiography."[4]

Now we will briefly survey the Old Testament, showing some of the historical and archaeological evidence that gives further testimony to the reliability of biblical events. We will separate our survey into three major historical periods: the Middle Bronze Age (1950-1550 B.C.), the Late Bronze Age (1550-1200 B.C.), and the Iron Age (1200-330 B.C.).

The Middle Bronze Age

Old Testament scholar D. J. Wiseman shows how archaeology has helped confirm early biblical history from the Middle Bronze Age:

"The Patriarchs fit best into the early Middle Bronze Age (MBA I), though their association with the Amorites or other folk-movements (including early Hapiru) known from contemporary texts cannot be proved. The Genesis narrative accords well with the archaeologically known occupation of the city-states that were then a dominant feature of Palestine. The occupation of Bethel, Shechem, Hebron (Kirjath-Arba), and the Dead Sea region of Sodom and Gomorrah is confirmed, as is that of the Negeb in southwest Palestine where flocks and herds (cf. Genesis 18:7; 20:1; 24:62) and grain crops (Genesis 26:12; 37:7) are traced in MBA I. There is valuable evidence of the verisimilitude [quality of appearing to be true] of the patriarchal personal and place names at this time. Thus, the name "Abram" occurs in a text from Dilbat *(Aba[m]rama)* and Aburahana (Abraham) and Zabilan (Zebulon) in Egyptian execration texts. Turahi (Terah), Nahur (Nahor), Sarugi (Serug), Laban, and Mar (Ben)-Yamin (Bejamin) are in eighteenth-century texts from Mari with reference to the Harran area and Ya'qub-il (Jacob) from nearby Chagar-Bazar. Other texts from these towns and from Alalah (from the eighteenth to the fifteenth century), Ur, Ras Shamra (fourteenth century), and Nuzi in Assyria (fifteenth century) throw considerable light on the patriarchal social customs. It can be seen that it was usual for a childless couple to adopt an heir and then displace him in the event of the birth of a real son (Genesis 15:4). According to her marriage contract, a barren woman was to provide her husband with a slave-girl to bear a son. Marriages were arranged for public purposes by the rulers of Ugarit and Qatna, as well as by Egyptian kings, and this may be reflected in the adventures [sic] of Sarah (Gen 20) and Rebekah (Gen 26). The special position of the first-born son (cf. Gen. 21:10ff; 48:14ff.), the bridegroom "asking" for a daughter as bride, the use of betrothal and bride-gifts (Gen 34:12), and the stipulation of marriage-contracts that a man might take a third wife only if the first two were barren or take a second wife only if the first failed to give birth within seven years explain incidents in Genesis."[5]

The premier biblical archaeologist of all time, William F. Albright, confirmed the historical and archaeological accuracy of the Old Testament during the patriarchal period:

"Until recently it was the fashion among biblical historians to treat the patriarchal sagas of Genesis as though they were artificial creations of Israelite scribes of the Divided Monarchy or tales told by imaginative rhapsodists around Israelite campfires during the centuries following their

occupation of the country. Eminent names among scholars can be cited for regarding every item of Gen. 11-50 as reflecting late invention, or at least retrojection of events and conditions under the Monarchy into the remote past, about which nothing was thought to have been really known to the writers of later days.

"...Archaeological discoveries since 1925 have changed all this. Aside from a few die-hards among older scholars, there is scarcely a single biblical historian who has not been impressed by the rapid accumulation of data supporting the substantial historicity of patriarchal tradition. According to the traditions of Genesis the ancestors of Israel were closely related to the semi-nomadic peoples of Trans-Jordan, Syria, the Euphrates basin and North Arabia in the last centuries of the second millennium B.C., and the first centuries of the first millennium.[6]

Mosaic of Daniel the prophet.

Furthermore, modern day scholarship has shown that the early biblical accounts are unique in their composition.

All who suspect or suggest borrowing by the Hebrews are compelled to admit large-scale revision, alteration, and reinterpretation in a fashion which cannot be substantiated for any other composition from the ancient Near East or in any other Hebrew writing....Careful comparison of ancient texts and literary methods is the only way to the understand-

103

ing of the early chapters of Genesis. Discovery of new material requires reassessment of former conclusions; so the Epic of Atrahasis adds to knowledge of parallel Babylonian traditions, and of their literary form. All speculation apart, it underlines the uniqueness of the Hebrew primeval history in the form in which it now exists.[7]

Kenneth Kitchen, the Egyptian scholar, echoes these thoughts:

The common assumption that the Hebrew account is simply a purged and simplified version of the Babylonian legend (applied also to the Flood stories) is fallacious on methodological grounds. In the Ancient Near East, the rule is that simple accounts or traditions may give rise (by accretion

and embellishment) to elaborate legends, but not vice versa. In the ancient Orient, legends were not simplified or turned into pseudo-history (historicized) as has been assumed for early Genesis.[8]

The Late Bronze Age

The Late Bronze Age deals with the period from 1550-1200 B.C. This is one of the areas in which archaeology has been able to confirm the conquest of Canaan by the Israelites. The Bible records that Joshua conquered Canaan through a series of battles.

In the past many liberal scholars believed that the Israelites slowly and peacefully infiltrated the central hill country of Canaan. Those scholars rejected the biblical account. Paul Lapp gives the background of the situation.

"The [Canaan] conquest provides another example of the search for connections between biblical and historical-archaeological material. This concerns an event for which there is a considerable amount of archaeological evidence, a great amount of detailed description in the biblical sources, and volumes of diverse opinions and hypotheses produced by modern scholars."[9]

Excavation in the cities of Bethel, Lachish and Debir showed that the biblical account was correct. Canaan was taken through conquest; all of those sites revealed destruction around 1200 B.C. Lapp concludes:

Michelangelo's Moses (Church of St. Peters in Vincoli, Rome).

"The archaeological evidence supports the view that the biblical traditions developed from an actual historical conquest under Joshua in the late thirteenth century B.C."[10]

The Iron Age

Since the Iron Age is so much closer to our time period, there is much more historical and archaeological evidence in support of the biblical events recorded of that time period (1200-330 B.C.). Below we have reproduced a summary of significant archaeological finds confirming biblical narratives:

"From this period onward, historical confirmation of the OT narratives is a much simpler matter, due to the comparative availability of extrabiblical evidence. The inscribed stele of Benhadad I, found in 1940 at a north Syrian site, has furnished general confirmation of the Syrian list in 1 Kings 15:18, without, however, identifying the Rezon who founded the Damascene dynasty or being specific about the number of Benhadads who ruled in Damascus. The discovery of the Moabite Stone in 1868 illustrated the vigor that Omri of Israel (c. 880-873 B.C.) displayed toward neighboring nations, and not least toward the Moabites. At this time Israel was referred to in Assyrian records at *Bit-Humri* (House of Omri), a designation that was also applied to Samaria, the royal captital. Omri's successors were known as *mar-Humri* or 'offspring of Omri.' 'Ahab the Israelite' was mentioned in the Monolith Inscription of Shalmaneser III (c. 858-824 B.C.) as the leader of a powerful military group, while the Black Obelisk of Shalmaneser, found by Layard at Nimrud in 1946, depicted Jehu, or his representative, kneeling submissively before the Assyrian king and offering tribute.

"A jasper seal found by Schumacher at Megiddo in 1904 and inscribed 'Shema, servant of Jeroboam' almost certainly refers to Jeroboam II (c. 781-743 B.C.). The Khorsabad annals of Sargon II (c. 772-705) recorded the fall of the northern kingdom in 722, while two decades later the Assyrian invasion of Judah, which resulted in Hezekiah's becoming tributary, was described in the annals of Sennacherib. The discovery in 1880 of a tunnel leading from the pool of Siloam and containing an inscription written in eighth-century B.C. script (c. 701) amply confirmed the activity mentioned in 2 Kings 20:20 and 2 Chronicles 32:30. The Canaanite characters of the Siloam Inscription are particularly valuable because of the scarcity of contemporary material written in Hebrew.

The discovery of D. J. Wiseman in 1956 of four additional tablets of the Babylonian Chronicle in the archives of the British Museum provided the first extrabiblical confirmation of the capture of Jerusalem in 597 B.C., dating it precisely on the second of Adar (March 15-16). In addition to mentioning the defeat of the Egyptian forces at Carchemish in 605, the tablets preserved an account of a previously unrecorded battle between Egypt and Babylon in 601, in which both sides suffered heavy losses. This material thus confirms the OT tradition that Jerusalem fell to Babylon in 597 and again in 587."[11]

Clifford Wilson observes how archaeological discoveries have confirmed the biblical account of the Syrian invasion of Israel:
It is interesting that in 1 Chronicles 5:26 we read that God stirred up the spirit of Tiglath-pileser, king of Assyria, but he is also referred to there by the name Pul. At first this seems to be a mistake; then we look again and notice that a singular verb is used in association with the two names.

It turns out that Pullu was the throne name adopted by Tiglath-pileser when he became king of Babylon. He took this Babylonian name to avoid giving offense to the Babylonian people. The casual Bible reference is a remarkable piece of local color, and it is this sort of evidence that consistently reminds us that the Bible prophets and recorders lived against the backgrounds claimed for them. They confidently referred to kings and customs of the people with whom they and their leaders were in direct contact.

One of the most interesting confirmations of this general time period relates to the Assyrian king Sargon, referred to by name only in Isaiah

20:1. There we read that Sargon, the king of Assyria, sent his "tartan" (commander-in-chief) against the Philistine city of Ashdod, on the Mediterranean coast. Many Bible critics believed that this was clearly a mistake, for no King Sargon was known. Perhaps the reader can capture a bit of the excessively skeptical spirit in which such a reference would be dismissed simply because it is stated nowhere else. It was learnedly argued that King Shalmaneser must be meant, until Sargon's huge palace at Khorsabad was discovered. Not only that, but a wall description was found of the very battle referred to in Isaiah 20. Many years later there came further confirmation when the city of Ashdod was excavated. Archaeologists found three pieces of a broken memorial stele that turned out to be the boasting of Sargon about his capture and defeat of this Philistine city.

The Bible reference was substantiated and in fact demonstrated the reliability of the bible in no less than three different ways. It showed that there was a King Sargon, despite those critics who insisted there was no such king. Second, it confirmed the particular reference to a campaign by Sargon against Philistine Ashdod. Third, it showed that the Bible writers even knew the titles of the Assyrians with whom they were in frequent (though hostile) contact. Prophets such as Isaiah and Jeremiah confidently and always correctly used such titles as Tartan, Rabshakeh (chief officer). Rabsaris (chief treasurer), and Tupsarru (captain). Critics are frequently claiming that biblical texts are later than the dates the texts give for themselves. Yet, in spite of the fact that the Assyrians disappeared from history after the Battle of Carchemish in 605 B.C., these Bible writers even knew such intimate details as the titles of the enemy.

Let's change contexts for a moment. Who would know the titles of army officers in World War II, or in the wars fought in Korea or Vietnam? Only those who had been in those conflicts or who had direct contact with those who had been there. The way these Bible writers confidently and consistently use the titles of the enemy is a clear pointer to the fact that they were writing against the backgrounds claimed for them by the Bible.[12]

Some Reversals in Old Testament Criticism

Not only has the basic history of the Old Testament period been confirmed by archaeological testimony, there also have been some startling reversals of Old Testament criticism. Below are some examples.

The "Shrine of the Book" in which the valuable Dead Sea Scrolls are located.

Until this century with its archaeological discoveries, it was believed that Moses could not have written the first five books of the Old Testament because writing was said to be virtually unknown or at least not commonly used. Representative of this thought was liberal Hermann Schultz, who wrote in 1898:

"Of the legendary character of the pre-Mosaic narrators, the time of which they treat is a sufficient proof. It was a time prior to all knowledge of writing, a time separated by an interval of more than four hundred years, of which there is absolutely no history, from the nearest period of which Israel had some dim historical recollection, a time when in civilized countries writing was only beginning to be used for the most important matters of State. Now wandering herdsmen have invariably an instinctive dislike to writing. In fact, at the present day, it is considered a disgrace among many Bedouin tribes in the peninsula of Sinai to be able to write. It is therefore impossible that such men could hand down their family histories, in themselves quite unimportant, in any other way than orally, to wit, in legends. And even when writing had come into use, in the time, that is, between Moses and David, it would be but sparingly used, and much that happened to the people must still have been handed down simply as legend."[13]

Note the use of such terms as "impossible" and "legend." The consensus was that Moses could not have written the first five books of the Old Testament because of the lack of the widespread use of writing or his lack of interest in recording Israel's history.

Modern historical and archaeological discoveries, however, show that writing was in common use prior to the time of Moses. It is clear that Moses had the capacity to write the first five books. D. J. Wiseman observes:

"Well before the end of the second millenium the pressures of trade and need for communication led to the widespread use of this simple form of writing (e.g., in marking personal objects; cf. stone inscriptions of Ahiram). Thus, by the time of the entry of the Hebrews into Canaan in the Late Bronze Age they would be confronted, if not already familiar, with at least five different forms of writing systems used for eight or more languages: (1) Egyptian hieroglyphs (Beth-shan, Chinnereth); (2) the Byblos syllabic script; (3) 'Proto-Hebrew' (Lachish, Hazor); (4) Akkadian (Mesopotamian) cuneiform; and (5) the Ugaritic alphabetic script (found also at Beth-Shemesh)."[14]

This is echoed by an Old Testament authority, Cyrus Gordon, who wrote:

"The excavations at Ugarit have revealed a high material and literary culture in Canaan prior to the emergence of the Hebrews. Prose and poetry were already fully developed. The educational system was so advanced that dictionaries in four languages were compiled for the use of scribes, and the individual words were listed in their Ugaritic, Babylonian,

Sumerian, and Hurrian equivalents. The beginnings of Israel are rooted in a highly cultural Canaan where the contributions of several talented peoples (including the Mesopotamians, Egyptians, and branches of the Indo-Europeans) had converged and blended. The notion that early Israelite religion and society were primitive is completely false. Canaan in the days of the Patriarchs was the hub of a great international culture. The Bible, hailing from such a time and place, cannot be devoid of sources. But let us study them by taking the Bible on its own terms and against its own authentic background."[15]

Archaeology is occupied with serious and scientific investigation of old cultures. It has long since ceased to be a sort of treasure-hunting.

One of the most startling confirmations of the historical accuracy of the Bible during the patriarchal period concerns Genesis 14. For many years Genesis 14 was assumed to be unhistorical. Archaeologist William F. Albright even wrote that "the Hebrew material was either borrowed from extant legends like the saga of the cities of the plain and the legend of Melchizedek, or invented by use of haggadic processes."[16]

However, as Albright himself discovered later, there is evidence that confirms the historicity of the biblical account. Albright later wrote:

"...this account represents the invading host as marching down from Hauran through eastern Gilead and Moab to the southeastern part of Palestine. Formerly this writer considered this extraordinary line of march as being the best proof of the essentially legendary character of the narrative. In 1929, however, he discovered a line of Early and Middle Bronze Age mounds, some of great size, running down along the eastern edge of Gilead, between the desert and the forest of Gilead. Moreover, the citiesof Hauran (Bashan) with which the account of the campaign opens, Ashtaroth and Karnaim, were both occupied in this period, as shown by archaeological examination of their sites. The same is true of eastern Moab, where the writer discovered an Early Middle-Bronze city at Ader in 1924. This route called 'The Way of the King,' in later Israelite tradition, does not appear to have ever been employed by invading armies in the Iron Age."[17]

The Hittites

The Hittites, mentioned some 50 times in the Old Testament, were considered for a long time to be a biblically fabricated people. That is, the biblical references to the Hittites used to be regarded as historically worthess. John Elder comments on modern confirmation of the Hittites:

Excavations have proven that the role of writing had been of great importance long before Moses. The civilizations of Egypt, Sumer, Akkad and Ebla possessed all kinds of written records. This is borne out by tens of thousands of clay tablets that have been found. This means that Moses could well have used older histories for the book of Genesis, written by the patriarchs and preserved with reverence by the people.

"...one of the striking confirmations of Bible history to come from the science of archaeology is the 'recovery' of the Hittite peoples and their empires. Here is a people whose name appears again and again in the Old Testament, but who in secular history had been completely forgotten and whose very existence was considered to be extremely doubtful.... In Genesis 23:10, it is told that Abraham bought a parcel of land for a burying place from Ephron the Hittite. In Genesis 26:34, Esau takes a Hittite girl for a wife, to the great grief of his mother. In the Book of Exodus, the Hittites are frequently mentioned in the lists of people whose land the Hebrews set out to conquer. In Joshua 11:1-9, the Hittites join in the confederation of nations that try to resist Joshua's advance, only to be defeated by the waters of Merom. In Judges, intermarriage occurs between the Hebrews and the Hittites. In 1 Samuel 26, Hittites enroll in David's army, and during the reign of Solomon he makes slaves of the Hittite element in his kingdom and allows his people to take Hittite wives. But until the investigations of modern archaeologists, the Hittites remained a shadowy and undefined people."[18]

Archaeologist A. H. Sayce was the first scholar to identify the Hittite people from a non-biblical source, the monuments. In 1876 he released his information and revolutionized critical theory concerning the Hittites.

Since Sayce's time in the last century, much information about the Hittites has been discovered, confirming again the historical accuracy of the Old Testament. Fred H. Wight concludes:

"Now the Bible picture of this people fits in perfectly with what we know of the Hittite nation from the monuments. As an empire they never conquered the land of Canaan itself, although Hittite local tribes did settle there at an early date. Nothing discovered by the excavators has in any way discredited the Biblical account. Scripture accuracy has once more been proved by the archaeologists."[19]

Summary and Conclusion

After examining some of the historical and archaeological evidence in favor of the historical reliability of the Old Testament, we conclude with several observations:

1. The persons, places and events listed during the different periods of Old Testament history match up well with the facts and evidence from history and archaeology.

2. Recent developments in textual criticism give examples of reversals by liberal critics who dismissed Old Testament passages for lack of evidence and then were forced by new evidence to accept them as historically reliable.

3. It must be restated that we first believe the Old Testament to be historically reliable because of the testimony of Jesus Christ, God in human flesh, whose claims were validated by His resurrection from the dead and who endorsed the Old Testament as the Word of God. Old Testament authority John Bright summarized it like this:

"I am quite unable to get around the fact...that the Old Testament was authoritative Scripture for Jesus himself. Jesus knew no Scripture save the Old Testament, no God save its God; it was this God whom He addressed as Father.' True, He used the Scriptures with sovereign freedom, as befitted Him. But never once did He suggest that in the light of His work they might safely be discarded. On the contrary, He regarded the Scriptures as the key to the understanding of His person; again and again He is represented as saying that it is the Scriptures that witness to Him and are fulfilled in Him. At no place did He express Himself as shocked by the Old Testament, nor did He adopt...a polemical attitude toward it (though often enough toward the religious leaders of His day and their interpretations). I find it most interesting and not a little odd that although the Old Testament on occasion offends our Christian feelings, it did not apparently offend Christ's 'Christian feelings'! Could it really be that we are ethically and religiously more sensitive than He? Or is it perhaps that we do not view the Old Testament — and its God — as He did? The very fact that the Old Testament was normative Scripture to Jesus, from which He understood both His God and (however we interpret His self-consciousness) Himself, means that it must in some way be normative Scripture for us too — unless we wish to understand Jesus in some other way than He himself did and the New Testament did."[20]

Page 111: From the midst of a bush that burned, but was not consumed, God first revealed Himself to Moses (Exodus 3:1 to 4:17).

CHAPTER SEVEN

The Historical Reliability of the New Testament

Page 112: "Everyone who drinks of this water shall thirst again; but whoever drinks of the water that I shall give him shall never thirst; but the water that I shall give him shall become in him a well of water springing up to eternal life." (John 4:13,14).

On the right: The eternal life that Jesus gives, is the life that He Himself procured by His resurrection from the dead. Here a grave is cut out of the rock from the first century A.D.—a subterranean passage with a number of recesses that can be closed off with a large stone disc.

The New Testament is primarily a record of the salvation work of Jesus Christ, the Son of God. It is not primarily a historical record. Yet when the New Testament addresses itself to historical issues, it is accurate and reliable.

Much of the older New Testament criticism did not have the vital testimony of archaeological evidence available today. Archaeologist William F. Albright observed:

"...the form-critical school founded by M. Dibelius and R. Bultmann a generation before the discovery of the Dead Sea Scrolls has continued to flourish without the slightest regard for the Dead Sea Scrolls. In other words, all radical schools in New Testament criticism which have existed in the past or which exist today are prearchaeological, and are, therefore, since they were built *in der Luft* ['in the air'], quite antiquated today."[1]

This chapter reviews some of the important archaeological discoveries that confirm the New Testament view of the first-century world. We will first discuss the life and work of New Testament archaeologist/historian, Sir William Ramsey, and then review several important archaeological and historical finds that affirm the reliability of the New Testament.

Sir William Ramsey

Sir William Ramsey is an example of how an honest scholar of history

can change his entire presuppositional perspective when faced by incontrovertible evidence from history and archaeology. Ramsey began his historical research toward the end of the nineteenth century. When he began his research he based in on the German (Tubingen) liberal/critical school of thought, which taught that the New Testament was not written in the first century and was not historically reliable. Instead it was an invention of the second-century church. Although the New Testament book of Acts contained a variety of supposedly present-tense historical references, liberal critics rejected its historicity and declared it a fabrication.

As a young historian, Ramsey determined to develop an independent historical/geographical study of first-century Asia Minor. Assuming the unreliability of the book of Acts, he ignored its historical allusions in his studies. The amount of usable historical information concerning first-century Asia Minor, however, was too little for him to proceed very far with his work. That led him, almost in desperation, to consult the book of Acts. He discovered that it was remarkably accurate and true to first-century history and typography. Here are Ramsey's own words chronicling his change of mind:

"I may fairly claim to have entered on this investigation without prejudice in favour of the conclusion which I shall now seek to justify to the reader. On the contrary, I began with a mind unfavourable to it, for the ingenuity and apparent completeness of the Tubigen theory had at one time quite convinced me. It did not then lie in my line of life to investigate the subject minutely, but more recently I found myself brought into contact with the Book of Acts as an authority for the topography, antiquities and society of Asia Minor. It was gradually borne upon me that in various details the narrative showed marvelous truth. In fact, beginning with a fixed idea that the work was essentially a second century composition, and never relying on its evidence as trustworthy for first century conditions, I gradually came to find it a useful ally in some obscure and difficult investigations."[2]

Ramsey's studies led him to conclude that "Luke's history is unsurpassed in respect of its trustworthiness,"[3] and "Luke is a historian of the first rank; not merely are his statements of fact trustworthy...this author should be placed along with the very greatest of historians."[4] From the experience of Ramsey we see that the New Testament writer Luke, author of the greatest portion of the New Testament (Luke and Acts) and an eyewitness of many events during the growth of the first-century church, was a careful historian.

The fact that many historical details, national boundaries, and government structures in Asia Minor were different in the second century from what they had been in the first makes it still more reasonable to conclude that the accurate author of Luke and Acts was a first-century author, not a second-century one.

Acts 14:1-6, for example, was in disrepute historically for many years. The passage implies that Lystra and Derbe were in Lycaonia but Iconium was not. Later Roman writers (such as Cicero) contradicted the passage, asserting that Iconium was in Lycaonia. For years this was used by the critical school to show the historical unreliability of Acts.

In 1910, however, Sir William Ramsey discovered a first-century inscription declaring that the first-century Iconium was under the authority of Phrygia, not Lycaonia. It was only in the second century that territorial boundaries changed and Iconium came under Lycaonian rule. A first-century writer would be aware of this historical detail; a second-century writer could have been ignorant of it. Ramsey's discovery was another confirmation of the historical reliability of the New Testament.

The Census in the Gospel of Luke

For years New Testament critics denied the historical reliability of the account about the Roman census recorded in Luke 2. Critics saw this as an excuse invented for Mary and Joseph to be in Bethlehem at the birth of Jesus. They believed that second-century New Testament writers had to fabricate a fulfillment to the Old Testament prophecy that the

Jerusalem, the place where Abraham was willing to sacrifice his son Isaac (Genesis 22:1-19), is also the place where God did indeed sacrifice His Son for us.

Messiah was to be born in Bethlehem. Luke wrote:

"Now it came about in those days that a decree went out from Caesar Augustus, that a census be taken of all the inhabited earth. This was the first census taken while Quirinius was governor of Syria. And all were proceeding to register for the census, everyone to his own city. And Joseph also went up from Galilee, from the city of Nazareth, to Judea, to the city of David, which is called Bethlehem, because he was of the house and family of David, in order to register, along with Mary, who was engaged to him, and was with child."[5]

For many years there was no outside evidence of any census at that time. Jesus was born sometime before 4 B.C. A census was taken under Quirinius in A.D. 6 or 7, but there was no evidence for an earlier one that could correspond with the date of Jesus' birth. Many critics assumed that this was another historical error of some second-century writer who called himself Luke and claimed to have "checked his facts." However, what was eventually discovered revealed Luke's integrity and reflected poorly on the critics. Biblical scholar Gleason L. Archer chronicles the problem and its solution:

"Luke 2:1 tells of a decree from Caesar Augustus to have the whole 'world' *(oikoumene* actually means all the world under the authority of Rome) enrolled in a census report for taxation purposes. Verse 2 specifies which

115

census taking was involved at the time Joseph and Mary went down to Bethlehem, to fill out the census forms as descendants of the Bethlehemite family of King David. This was the first census undertaken by Quirinius (or 'Cyrenius') as governor (or at least as acting governor) of Syria. Josephus mentions no census in the reign of Herod the Great (who died in 4 B.C.) but he does mention one taken by 'Cyrenius' *(Antiquities* 17.13.5) soon after Herod Archelaus was deposed in A.D. 6: 'Cyrenius, one that had been consul, was sent by Caesar to take account of people's effects in Syria, and to sell the house of Archelaus.' (Apparently the palace of the deposed king was to be sold and the proceeds turned over to the Roman government.)

"If Luke dates the census in 8 or 7 B.C., and if Josephus dates it in A.D. 6 or 7, there appears to be a discrepancy of about fourteen years. Also, since Saturninus (according to Tertullian in *Contra Marcion* 4:19) was legate of Syria from 9 B.C. to 6 B.C., and Quintilius Varus was legate from 7 B.C. to A.D. 4 (note the one-year overlap in these two terms!), there is doubt as to whether Quirinius was ever governor of Syria at all.

"By way of solution, let it be noted first of all that Luke says this was a 'first' enrollment that took place under Quirinius *(haute apographe prote egeneto).* A 'first' surely implies a *second* one sometime later. Luke was therefore well aware of that second census, taken by Quirinius again in A.D. 7, which Josephus alludes to in the passage cited above. We know this because Luke (who lived much closer to the time than Josephus did) also quotes Gamaliel as alluding to the insurrection of Judas of Galilee 'in the days of the census taking' (Acts 5:27). The Romans tended to conduct a census every fourteen years, and so this comes out right for a first census in 7 B.C. and a second in A.D. 7.

"But was Quirinius (who was called *Kyrenius* by the Greeks because of the absence of a Q in the Attic alphabet, or else because this proconsul was actually a successful governor of Crete and Cyrene in Egypt around 15 B.C.) actually governor of Syria? The Lucan text here says, 'while Cyrenius was leading—in charge of—Syria' *(hegemoneuontos tes Syrias Kyreniou).* He is not actually called *legatus* (the official Roman title for the governor of an entire region). The grammatical structure used here would be appropriate to refer to Quirinius more as a procurator like Pontius Pilate but not as a legatus.

"Too much should not be made of the precise official status. But we do know that between 12 B.C. and 2 B.C., Quirinius was engaged in a systematic reduction of rebellious mountaineers in the highlands of Pisidia (Tenney, *Zondervan Pictorial Encyclopedia,* 5:6), and that he was therefore a highly placed military figure in the Near East in the closing years of the reign of Herod the Great. In order to secure efficiency and dispatch, it may well have been that Augustus put Quirinius in charge of the census-enrollment in the region of Syria just at the transition period between the close of Saturninus's administration and the beginning of Varus's term of service in 7 B.C. It was doubtless because of his competent handling of the 7 B.C. census that Augustus later put him in charge of the A.D. 7 census.

"As for the lack of secular reference to a general census for the entire Roman Empire at this time, this presents no serious difficulty. Kingsley Davis *(Encyclopaedia Britannica,* 14th ed., 5:168) states: 'Every five years

the Romans enumerated citizens and their property to determine their liabilities. This practice was extended to include the entire Roman empire in 5 B.C.'"[6]

(As a side comment, we also note that while liberal critics had in the past discounted the existence of proconsul Pontius Pilate, who gave the crucifixion order for Jesus Christ, A. Frova, an archaeologist, discovered an inscription concerning Pilate in 1961. The inscription was on a theater, at Caesarea, erected by Pilate in honor of Tiberius. The inscription commemorated the dedication of the structure and attributed it to Pilate, proconsul of Judea.)

The Burial Place of Jesus Christ

Another detail of New Testament history that has been confirmed concerns the burial place of Jesus Christ. Contemporary archaeologist and historian Dr. Edwin Yamauchi reports:

"The traditional site of Calvary and the associate tomb of Christ was desecrated by Hadrian in A.D. 135. In the fourth century, Helena, the mother of Constantine, was led to the site, where she then built the Church of the Holy Sepulchre. Excavations in and around the church have helped demonstrate that it lay outside the wall in Jesus' day. Shafts dug in the church show that the area was used as a quarry and was therefore extra-

117

mural, a conclusion also supported by Kenyon's excavations in the adjoining Muristan area. Thus there is no reason to doubt the general authenticity of the site.

"In the course of repairs since 1954 remains of the original Constantinian structure have been exposed. In 1975 M. Broshi found near St. Helena's chapel in the church a red and black picture of a Roman sailing ship and a Latin phrase *Domine iuimus*, 'Lord, we went' (cf. Ps. 122:1). These words and the drawing were placed there by a pilgrim A.D. 330.

"As for the actual tomb of Christ, quarrying operations may have obliterated the grave. A bench *arcosolium* (flat surface under a recessed

arch) must have been used for Jesus. But early Christian pilgrims seem to have seen a trough *arcololium* (rock-cut sarcophagus); this raises the question of whether they saw the actual tomb.

"In 1842 Otto Thenius, a German pastor, was attracted to a hill 150 yards north of the present walled city because of two cavities that give it a skull-like appearance. The hill was popularized among Protestants as an alternative site for Calvary by General Gordon in 1883. A seventeenth-century sketch of the hill demonstrates, however, that the cavities were not yet present then. The nearby 'Garden Tomb' likewise has no claim to be the authentic tomb of Christ."[7]

The Resurrection of Christ

On the resurrection, archaeology has a piece of astonishing evidence to offer, for it is quite beyond question that one of the most interesting archaeological discoveries in Palestine during the century of exploration its ancient sites have seen, is a simple slab of white marble from Nazareth, the hometown of Christ. The stone found its way in 1878 into the collection of a distinguished antiquarian named Froehner, who noted it down in his catalog simply thus: "Slab of marble sent from Nazareth in 1878."

Froehner was an eccentric person, but an arahaeologist of exact scholar-

118

ship and distinction, most unlikely to have been deceived. If he so recorded the origin of the Nazareth stone, the statement can be quite unreservedly accepted. As a collector, on the other hand, Froehner guarded his treasures jealously, and derived a perverse and lamentable enjoyment from the possession of antiquities of which the world of scholarship knew nothing. Publication, to Froehner's mind, diminished his personal interest in possession.

In the order of nature Froehner passed away, and the items of his fine collection found their way to the French treasure house of the Louvre. The piece of marble from Nazareth was housed in the Cabinet de Medailles, and at long last, in 1930 in fact, over half a century after its arrival in Europe, Michel Rostovtzeff, the great historian, cast his eye on its rather irregular lines of clear Greek script. He stared in astonishment, for here was an inscription of unique importance unknown to scholarship.

Page 118: A Greek-Orthodox monastery on Patmos, the island where the Apostle John received his revelation (Revelation 1:9).

This is what he read:

"Ordinance of Caesar. It is my pleasure that graves and tombs remain undisturbed in perpetuity for those who have made them for the cult of their ancestors, or children, or members of their house. If, however, any man lay information that another has either demolished them, or has in any other way extracted the buried, or has maliciously transferred them to other places in order to wrong them, or has displaced the sealing or other stones, against such a one I order that a trial be instituted, as in respect of the gods, so in regard to the cult of mortals. For it shall be much more obligatory to honor the buried. Let it be absolutely forbidden for anyone to disturb them. In the case of contravention I desire that the offender be sentenced to capital punishment on charge of violation of sepulture."

Need one stress the significance of a decree concerning moving the stone coverings of tombs, and extracting the bodies of the dead, which comes from the town where Christ lived? The scholars were not slow to move, and the Abbe Cumont, Rostovtzeff's friend, and a first-rate ancient historian, was quickly in the field with an account of the inscription, an attempt to date it, an analysis of the language, and an account of its significance.

Since the Abbe Cumont's article, which appeared in the *Journal of Hellenic Studies* in 1932, the field has become a well-trodden one, and it is a fact that every Roman emperor, from Augustus to Hadrian, with the exception of Caligula, has been named as the author of promulgator of the Nazareth Decree. No overwhelming reason, however, has been put forward for abandoning a position originally taken by Arnaldo Momigliano, the brillian Italian historian, who thought the decree a rescript of Claudius.[8]

The Letter of Mara Bar-Serapion

Secular testimony to the good reputation of Jesus Christ among non-Christians is available from very soon after His death and resurrection. Although Jesus Christ is not actually named in this portion of a first-century letter (c. A.D. 73 +), the context of the passage alludes to Him. This letter is housed in the British Museum. It is from a Syrian named Mara Bar-Serapion to his imprisoned son, Serapion, and is meant to encourage the son in his suffering. He gives no indication of knowing about or believing in the resurrection of Jesus Christ, but his letter does acknowledge Jesus' general character and historical existence:

"What advantage did the Athenians gain from putting Socrates to death? Famine and plague came upon them as a judgment for their crime. What advantage did the men of Samos gain from burning Pythagoras? In a moment their land was covered with sand. What advantage did the Jews gain from executing their King? It was just after that their kingdom was abolished. God justly avenged these three wise men: the Athenians died of hunger; the Samians were overwhelmed by the sea; the Jews, ruined and driven from their land, live in complete dispersion. But Socrates did

Solitude played an important role in Jesus' life: from the temptation in the wilderness (Matthew 4:1-11) to being absolutely forsaken by God and men on the cross (Matthew 27:45 and 46).

not die for good; he lived on in the teaching of Plato. Pythagoras did not die for good; he lived on in the statue of Hera. Nor did the wise King die for good; He lived on in the teaching which He had given."

The Accuracy of Luke

As earlier noted, Sir William Ramsay did much to substantiate that Luke was an accurate historian. E. M. Blaiklock comments:

Luke's meticulous care for the correct designation and definition is again and again apparent. When Paul crossed from Asia into Europe, Luke, his chronicler, on bringing the story to Philippi, described the town as "the first of the district." Even Hort marked this as a mistake, since the Greek word *meris* appeared never to be used for "region." The Egyptian papyri, however, revealed that Luke's Greek was better than that of his scholarly editor. The word, it was obvious, was quite commonly used for "district" in the first century, and especially in Macedonia.

But another difficulty remained. It has been demonstrated with some likelihood that Luke came from Philippi. Had enthusiasm for his hometown led the physician astray, for was not Amphipolis the local capital? Loyalty did play a part, and the amiable foible is a clear mark of Lucan authenticity. But there was no distortion of fact. "Afterwards,"

120

writes Ramsay, "Philippi quite outstripped its rival; but it was at that time in such a position that Amphipolis was ranked first by general consent, Philippi first by its own consent. These cases of rivalry between two or even three cities for the dignity and title of 'first' are familiar to every student of the history of the Greek cities; and though no other evidence is known to show that Philippi had as yet begun to claim the title, yet this single passage is conclusive. The descriptive phrase is like a lightning flash in the darkness of local history, revealing in startling clearness the whole situation to those whose eyes are trained to catch the character of Greek city-history. . ." It is odd to see the personality of the historian peep out. And what, in the light of it, of the rash theory of second-century

"The Three Crosses,"
etching by Rembrandt,
1653 (Rijksprentenkabinet,
Amsterdam).

romancing?

Luke also calls the local officials of Philippi "praetors." The term seemed incorrect until inscriptions established the fact that the title was a courtesy one for the magistrates of the Roman colony; and as usual Luke uses the term commonly employed in educated circles.[9]

In Romans 16:23 the apostle Paul wrote, "Erastus, the city treasurer greets you." Paul was writing from the Greek city of Corinth and by mentioning a city official, he has given us an opportunity to search records and archaeological data from Corinth in an attempt to confirm that official's existence and Paul's ability to record history accurately. Archaeological data, in fact, has been found to buttress the historical reliability of Paul's writings, so integral to the New Testament as a whole. Biblical scholar F. F. Bruce writes:

"Writing his Epistle to the Romans from Corinth during the winter of A.D. 56-57, Paul sends greetings from some of his companions, and adds: 'Erastus the City Treasurer greets you' (Rom. xvi. 23). In the course of excavations in Corinth in 1929, Professor T. L. Shear found a pavement with the inscription ERASTVS PRO : AED : S : P : STRAVIT ('Erastus, curator of public buildings, laid this pavement at his own expense'). The evidence indicates that this pavement existed in the first century A.D. and

121

it is most probable that the donor is identical with the Erastus who is mentioned by Paul."[10]

Classics professor E. M. Blaiklock has also commented on archaeological discoveries in Corinth that confirm New Testament historicity:

"It was Caesar's Corinth which Paul visited almost a century later still, and where, in the midst of the polyglot and cosmopolitan population of a notoriously vicious port, he founded the most troublesome and difficult of his Christian communities. It is also Caesar's Corinth on which the archaeologists have worked so busily, uncovering the agora, or market place, and part of the two roads which run down to Lechaeum, the port on the Corinthian Gulf, and Cenchrea, the twin landing place on the Aegean side of the isthmus. On the Lechaeum road a fragmentary inscription marks the synagogue of the Jews, where Paul preached. Across one end of the excavated market place runs a stone platform, six to seven feet high, and faced with marble. It is the *bema* where Gallio, Seneca's brother, sat to hear the case of Paul. His governorship incidentally, is dated A.D. 52 by an inscription at Delphi. A tantalizing block of marble found near the theater, bears another fragmentary inscription which reads: 'Erastus, for the office of aedile, laid this pavement at his own expense.' Is this Erastus, the city treasurer, who was a foundation member of the Corinthian church?"[11]

Finally, K. A. Kitchen, lecturer in Egyptian and Coptic in the School of Archaeology and Oriental Studies at the University of Liverpool, assesses the impact of modern archaeological and historical findings on the reliability of the writings of Luke and mentions the significance of the inscription of Erastus:

"Luke's writings are not alone in being sober records of reality, archaeologically speaking. The repute of Herod the Great as a builder, at the stones of whose temple Jesus's disciples and others marvelled (Luke 21-5; cf. John 2:20) has been fully borne out by recent work at Jerusalem at the site of the temple enclosure, and by work at his fortress-palaces elsewhere, as at Herodium and Masada. From Corinth to Rome, Paul sent greetings in his letter to the Romans, including from Erastus the treasurer (Romans 16:23). The selfsame individual was most probably the donor of a pavement of the first century A.D. at Corinth, inscribed in the name of one Erastus, curator of public buildings. And so on. Not surprisingly, trained historians of the Graeco-Roman world have repeatedly commented favourably upon the high historical value of the New Testament writings, and of Luke-Acts especially. Needless to say, problems of interpretation in detail exist in this field just as in any other, but are not necessarily insoluble. Certainly the evidence derived from this field of study calls into question the groundless scepticism underlying much German New Testament scholarship, based as it is (like its Old Testament counterpart) upon hypothetical theories of form criticism, redaction 'history' of the writings and so on, unrelated to observed literary usage in the surrounding world. Even in a 'visionary' book like Revelation, one may perceive the subtle undertones that relate the letters to the seven churches (Revelation 2-3) to the local features and background. Thus, for example, Laodicea was a rich banking-centre in a fertile countryside at an important junction of routes in Roman Asia. It lacked, however, a direct water-supply. Therefore its supplies had to be piped some distance from the hot springs, and were probably disappointingly lukewarm on

122

arrival at the city-end, 'neither hot nor cold' (cf. Revelation 3:14-22, esp. 16)."[12]

The Pool of Bethesda

John 5:1-14 tells of a miraculous healing performed by Jesus Christ at the pool of Bethesda. The story states that people in need of healing lay by the five porticoes or porches, waiting for an angel to stir the waters of the pool, at which time the ill could be healed. Jesus healed a man there merely by his word. For hundreds of years the location of the pool had been lost. Some doubted if it ever existed. Biblical scholar F. F. Bruce describes how this pool was found:

The Dead Sea Scrolls, found in the caves of Qumran, show that the text of the Old Testament has been reliably passed on to us.

"The pool of Bethesda, described in John [5:2], has been located in the north-east quarter of the old city of Jerusalem, the quarter which was called Bezetha, or 'New Town,' in the first century A.D. In 1888 excavations near St. Anne's Church, in that quarter, revealed the remains of an ancient church building. Beneath this lay a crypt, with its north wall divided into five compartments in imitation of arches; on this wall there could also be distinguished traces of an old fresco representing the angel troubling the water. Clearly those who built this structure believed that it marked the site of the pool of Bethesda. And subsequent excavations below the crypt showed that they were right; a flight of steps was uncovered leading down to a pool with five shallow porticoes on its north side, directly underneath the five imitation arches on the north wall of the crypt. There are few sites in Jerusalem, mentioned in the Gospels, which can be identified so confidently."[13]

Historian Dr. Edwin Yamauchi gives some corroborative information regarding the archaeological find of the pool of Bethesda:

"In Jerusalem there are two pools of water which can with confidence be associated with Jesus' ministry. The first is the Pool of Siloam (John 9:7-11) to which Jesus sent a blind man. The pool is located at the end of Hezekiah's tunnel. The other pool is that of Bethesda, a pool with

123

five porches or porticoes, at the side of which the lame man lay whom Jesus made whole (John 5:1-14). Early pilgrims had referred to the twin pools of Bethesda but over the centuries their location was lost. Then in 1888 as the White Fathers cleared some ruins on the grounds of the Church of St. Anne, they found an old fresco representing the story of John 5. Below this a flight of steps led down to the pools of Bethesda. Originally this had five porticoes, four on each side and a fifth separating the twin pools. It has been estimated that in Jesus' day the pools were as large as a football field, and about twenty feet deep."[14]

Summary and Conclusion

Jesus said: "I am the good shepherd; the good shepherd lays down his life for the sheep (John 10:11).

After reviewing some highlights of the overwhelming evidence supporting the historical reliability of the New Testament, we can come to the following conclusions:

1. Archaeological and historical evidence concerning the historical events, places, names and concepts mentioned in the New Testament conclusively affirms the basic historical reliability of the text. In addition the nature of much of the evidence supports the biblical assertion that the New Testament writers wrote during the first century and were either eyewitnesses of the events they described, or had carefully checked the facts and evidence with eyewitnesses. Luke reminds us of this concern for historical accuracy:

2. Not only are the New Testament authors accurate in their general historical observations, they are also accurate and meticulous in their recording of details. K. A. Kitchen highlights this concern for accurate detail:

"Turning from the text itself to its content, again, the general picture is a remarkably rich one. Ever since the Anatolian explorations and discoveries of (Sir) William Ramsey earlier this century, the accuracy of Luke as a historian and reporter has been upheld by a multiplicity of details, particularly in the book of Acts. He assigns the right titles to the proper officials at the correct periods of time in question. Such are

124

the proconsul in Cyprus (Acts 13:7) and of Achaia (Acts 18:12), the Asiarchs at Ephesus (Acts 19:31), among others. Back in Palestine, among Herod's heirs, Luke was careful to entitle Herod Antipas the *Tetrarch* of Galilee, not loosely 'king' as many of his subjects flatteringly did."[16]

3. Such concern for accuracy in general and in particular, which is exhibited by the New Testament writers for their historical accounts, is commensurate with a fidelity for truth in matters of teachings, morals, and spiritually significant issues. While historical accuracy does not guarantee such fidelity, it is a correlative necessity that one who claims to bring

"But for you who fear My name the sun of righteousness will rise with healing in its wings" (Malachi 4:2).

truth should tell the truth in all matters with which he or she deals. We should expect no less than historical accuracy from those who wrote the New Testament and claimed to represent the one who is the Way, the Truth, and the Life (John 14:6). As the apostle Peter said:

"For we did not follow cleverly devised tales when we made known to you the power and coming of our Lord Jesus Christ, but we were eyewitnesses of His majesty."[17]

4. If we accept the promise of Jesus Christ to send the Holy Spirit as our guide, teacher and comforter, then we should not be surprised that the Holy Spirit guided the disciples and New Testament writers. "But the Helper, the Holy Spirit, whom the Father will send in My name, He will teach you all things, and bring to your remembrance all that I said to you" (John 14:26). That biblical pattern of revelation is recorded in the book of Hebrews:

"God, after He spoke long ago to the fathers in the prophets in many portions and in many ways, in these last days has spoken to us in His Son, whom He appointed heir of all things, through whom also He made the world. And He is the radiance of His glory and the exact representation of His nature, and upholds all things by the word of His power."[18]

This short review of the historical reliability of the New Testament has made clear that we can trust the New Testament text in its general observations, conclusions and minute details. Such accuracy is consistent with the inspiration and fidelity to truth claimed for the writers of the New Testament.

125

CHAPTER EIGHT

The Contents of the Old Testament

We have shown that both the Old and New Testaments have been preserved accurately throughout history. We have also seen that historical events, well-known persons, and first-century places have been accurately documented. We have gone a step further and shown that there are definite reasons to believe that the Bible is more than an accurate historical document. Rather, it is the Word of God. The contents of the Bible are therefore of utmost importance. Chapters eight and nine will give a short summary of each of the books of the Bible in order to familiarize readers with the contents as well as give the historical flow of the biblical narration. That way it can be seen clearly what the Word of God teaches human beings about our meaning and our destiny. It will also help us to see God's sovereignty in history.

The following chart lists the books of the Old Testament in the order found in the English Bible. The human authorship of some books is uncertain, the dates given are approximate.

Book	Author	Approximate Date of Composition (B.C.)
Genesis	Moses	1440
Exodus	Moses	1440
Leviticus	Moses	1440
Numbers	Moses	1410
Deuteronomy	Moses	1410
Joshua	Joshua	1350
Judges	Samuel	1250
Ruth	Samuel	1250
1 and 2 Samuel	Compiled	1050
1 and 2 Kings	Compiled	800
1 and 2 Chronicles	Compiled	450
Ezra	Ezra	450
Nehemiah	Nehemiah	450
Esther	Mordecai?	550
Job	Moses?	1450
Psalms	David and various authors	550
Proverbs	Solomon	950
Ecclesiastes	Solomon	950
Song of Solomon	Solomon	950
Isaiah	Isaiah	675
Jeremiah	Jeremiah	580
Lamentations	Jeremiah	586
Ezekiel	Ezekiel	570

Page 126: The Bible begins in the book of Genesis with the description of the creation of the heavens and the earth.

Daniel	Daniel	530
Hosea	Hosea	725
Joel	Joel	830
Amos	Amos	755
Obadiah	Obadiah	845
Jonah	Jonah	760
Micah	Micah	725
Nahum	Nahum	654
Habakkuk	Habakkuk	606
Zephaniah	Zephaniah	621
Haggai	Haggai	520
Zechariah	Zechariah	475
Malachi	Malachi	435

After the flood, God chooses a people for Himself. He calls Abraham, who takes his sheep and goats and, with all his servants, leaves Ur of the Chaldees, in order to travel to the promised land.

Genesis

The book of Genesis is one of the most important books in the Bible. Genesis means *beginning* and this is the record of beginnings: the universe, human beings, animals, sin, and so on.

Creation

Genesis introduces an infinite and personal God who created all things: "In the beginning God created the heavens and the earth" (1:1). The crown of God's creation was man and woman whom God made in His own image (1:26, 27).

The Fall

Genesis describes how humanity failed in its responsibility, rebelled against God, and became totally dependent on His mercy (3). The rebellion that occurred placed a separation of sin between God and humankind. God therefore promised that a Savior would someday be sent to bring man back into a perfect relationship with God. Until that Savior would come along, God instituted a sacrificial system that would be a symbol of what Jesus Christ would later do to enable human beings to approach God. Jesus Christ eventually would appear as savior, providing Himself as the ultimate sacrifice.

The Flood

After the human fall into sin occurred, everyone continued to do evil. God decided to destroy all the earth's inhabitants, except faithful Noah and his family, by a great flood (6-9). After the flood, there was a new beginning; but humanity continued to rebel, symbolized by the forbidden building of the Tower of Babel (11). God spread humankind throughout the earth by confounding the languages people spoke.

The Abrahamic Covenant

After the Tower of Babel incident, God established a covenant with one man named Abraham, whom He called out from an idolatrous culture for the purpose of establishing a great and special nation (12:1-3). God also promised Abraham a land that would belong forever to his descendants (12-25). The rest of the book of Genesis deals with the descendants of Abraham: Isaac (21-27), Jacob (25-50) and Jacob's twelve sons, from whom came the 12 tribes of Israel. The book of Genesis closes with Jacob and his 12 sons in the land of Egypt, waiting for the fullfillment of God's promises.

Exodus

The book of Exodus records how Jacob's descendants began to multiply, thus fulfilling God's promise that a great nation would descend from Abraham. A pharaoh arose in Egypt who was threatened by the great number of the people of Israel and made slaves of them.

Deliverance

The people cried out to God to deliver them from this Egyptian bondage. God heard their cry and raised up Moses as their deliverer. The pharaoh did not want to let the people leave Egypt to go to the Promised Land, so God brought ten plagues upon Egypt (7-12). The last plague finally resulted in pharaoh's allowing the Israelites' *exodus,* or going out, from Egypt. Through that plague, Israel was reminded of the need for blood to be shed as the basis of forgiveness of sin (12). In instituting the *Passover,* God passed over and did not punish families in houses that had blood placed on the doorpost. The houses that did not have blood on the doorpost lost their firstborn sons through God's judgment. After the children of Israel left Egypt, they were miraculously delivered by God from the pursuing Egyptian army at the Red Sea (14).

Giving of the Law

Under God's protection they arrived at Mt. Sinai (13-19), where, through Moses, God gave them the Law, including the Ten Commandments (20). The Law would be the perfect standard of God, teaching the people that they could not measure up to what God required of them on their own and demonstrating their need for God's mercy and forgiveness. Exodus also records the laws of social and religious life that God's people were to observe (20-24).

Before the descendants of Abraham, the people of Israel, can enter the promised land, they must first spend 400 years of slavery in Egypt, followed by 40 years wandering in the wilderness.

The Tabernacle

God then gave Moses the design of a tent *(tabernacle)* which he was to build. The tabernacle would be a holy place, representing God's dwelling in the midst of His special people. Through the priest the people could approach God with their sacrifices (25-31). The tabernacle and its furnishings symbolized the person and work of the Messiah who was to come. The need for God's grace became evident during this time when the people rebelled; they designed and worshiped a golden calf. Moses interceded with God on their behalf, and most of them were saved from God's just wrath (32-33). The tabernacle was then built, solemnly dedicated, and

Canaan, the promised land, looks appealing enough to them, but the people do not believe that God is able to give it to them. This is a section from a painting by Nicolaas Poussin showing the astonishment of the sojourners in the wilderness as they see the good land, but also the power of the enemies living in it.

was visibly filled with the glory of God (40).

Leviticus

The book of Leviticus records the instructions God gave Moses at the door of his tent on Mt. Sinai. God first gave instruction about five offerings the people were to present to God: the burnt offering, the grain offering, the peace offering, the sin offering and the trespass offering (1-7). Then Aaron and his sons were consecrated as the priests who would present these offerings (8-10).

Laws and Regulations

After that, God gave further laws dealing with purity (11-22). These laws tell what food was to be eaten and what was not, along with regulations for a pure nation, pure marriages, pure morals and pure priests. Following this section are the laws of the feasts (23-25). Israel's seven high holy days are explained. The book closes with special laws on blessings and cursing, taking vows and giving of tithes (26-27).

Numbers

The book of Numbers deals with the journeys of the children of Israel on their way to the Promised Land. A census of the people was taken, and the tribes were arranged for traveling, with particular attention being given to the priests (1-4). Laws were given for the purity of the camp (5-6) and for the offerings for worship (7-8). The remembrance of the Passover was celebrated for the first time since the Israelites left Egypt, and God supernaturally guided His people with a cloud by day and a pillar of fire by night (9). Special signals were given the people for marching and assembling (10).

Complaints and Unbelief

As the people began their journey, they continually complained against God (10-12). Reaching the borders of the Promised Land, 12 spies were sent out; all except Joshua and Caleb brought back a negative report, which caused the people to complain even more. God punished this unbelief by sending them to wander aimlessly 40 years through the wilderness, with everyone over 20 years of age, except Joshua and Caleb, dying in the desert (13-14). During this period Moses and Aaron also sinned and were forbidden by God to enter the Promised Land.

Years of Wandering

The remainder of the book chronicles the events of the period of wandering, including the rebellion of Korah (16) and the plague of serpents sent upon the camp for unbelief (21). Israel, with God's help, conquered the Midianites while coming again to the borders of the Promised Land. The tribes of Reuben, Gad, and half the tribe of Manasseh preferred to settle on the east side of the Jordan River rather than to enter the Promised Land (31-32). The book closes with a review of the years of wandering and precautionary instructions to the people about the conquest and division of the Promised Land (33-36).

Deuteronomy

Deuteronomy is known as the Second Law. It contains the final words of Moses, probably delivered during the last week of his life. It is not merely a repetition of the Law, but rather an application of it as the people were about to possess the Land of Promise. Moses began by reviewing the history of the 40 years of wandering in the wilderness since leaving Egypt (1-4).

Laws for the New Land

He repeated and elaborated on the Ten Commandments, preparing the people for obeying them in the new land (4-11). He continued with the repetition of other laws that would have special application in the Promised Land: laws about idolatry, the eating of meat, the Sabbatical year, the feasts and the administration of justice (12-18). There is also a prophecy about a special prophet who would come (18). Laws were given dealing with criminals, the military, and civil responsibility. Moses concluded his discourse with directions about the thank offering of the "first fruits" to the Lord (26). He gave instructions on how the Law was to be confirmed upon entering the land (27-30).

Prophecies

This last discourse is one of the most important sections in Scripture: it prophesies the future course of the nation of Israel. Through Moses, God spoke of the blessing His people would receive as long as they remained obedient; He warned of judgments to come if they disobeyed. God promised that disobedience would cause removal of their land and a scattering of the people among the nations. However, faithful to His promises, God would bring a remnant back to the land. This prophecy has been fulfilled twice in Israel's history. The first removal was completed in 586 B.C., with a remnant returning in 536 B.C. The second time the people were scattered was in A.D. 70 with the remnant returning as a nation almost 1,900 years later, in May 1948. History has borne out the fact that God is true to His Word. The remainder of Deuteronomy (31-33) records the appointing of Joshua as Moses' successor, a song, and

David confessing his guilt before God. "Against Thee, Thee only, I have sinned" (Pslam 51:4).

a prophetic blessing given by Moses to the nation, mentioning each tribe. The final chapter (34) records Moses' death.

Joshua

The book of Deuteronomy closes with the Israelites about to enter the Promised Land. The book of Joshua describes how the Israelites entered Canaan, under Moses' successor Joshua and began to conquer it. Joshua led the children of Israel across the Jordan River after sending out spies to explore the land. The crossing of the Jordan occurred in a miraculous fashion, with flood waters rolling back to let the people, led by those carrying the Ark of the Covenant, cross to the other side. Two monuments were erected (one in the riverbed and another right beside it) to commemorate this event. The males were circumcised, something neglected during the wilderness wanderings, and the first Passover in the Promised Land was celebrated.

Occupying the New Land

The city of Jericho was the first to be conquered. The next city to be taken was Ai, but not until after the Israelites suffered a resounding defeat because of the sin of Achan (6-8).

Then followed the solemn confirmation of the Law in accordance with the instructions given by Moses. The ungodly inhabitants living in the south and north were destroyed; only the people of Gibeon escaped, because of a clever trick they pulled on the Israelites (8-12). The land was then divided among the remaining nine and a half tribes, with faithful Caleb given a special portion (13-19). Within the land itself, and also east of the Jordan River, a number of cities were designated "Cities of Refuge," designed to give refuge to anyone who unintentionally committed manslaughter. Forty-eight cities were set aside for the priestly class, the Levites (20-21). The two and a half tribes erected an altar across the Jordan against God's designation of the Jordan as the boundary of the Promised Land (23).

Model of Herod's Temple, the third temple built. The first temple had been built by Solomon; the second, after the Babylonian captivity, was erected under Zerubbabel.

Joshua's Charge

Joshua then addressed the people and charged them to keep God's Law. The covenant was renewed. The book closes with the death of Joshua.

Judges

The book of Judges covers a 300-year period between the death of Joshua and the institution of the monarchy in Israel. This was one of the darkest periods in Israel's history. During this time the people were ruled by judges, or magistrates, who not only administered justice, but also delivered Israel from its enemies. A cycle that happened seven times in the book of Judges went like this: the people were in fellowship with God, then fell into idolatry. Consequently, they were conquered by another people, which made them cry out to God for help. God heard their cry and sent a judge to deliver them and restore them to fellowship. Then the cycle began again.

Incomplete Conquest

The book begins with the Angel of the Lord coming from Gilgal to Bochim to rebuke the people for not driving the enemies completely out of the land. The conquest of the land was incomplete—one of Israel's most troublesome enemies, the Philistines, were allowed by the Israelites to live within the borders of the land in violation of the direct command of God. Consequently there was a need for a judge.

Led by Judges

The judges for the most part were insignificant people, not known for their greatness. One of the most courageous was a woman named Deborah (4-5). Other judges included Gideon, who defeated a great company of Midianites with only 300 men (6-9); Jephthah, who made a rash vow (10-12); and Samson, who completely wasted the powers given him by God (13-16).

Spiritual Chaos

The last part of the book (17-21) describes the introduction of idolatry into the tribe of Dan and a horrible deed done to the tribe of Benjamin. All these were because of the Israelites' failure to obey the commandments of God and because of the lack of strong leadership during this period. The last verse of the book sums up the era; "In those days there was no king in Israel; everyone did what was right in his own eyes" (21:25).

Ruth

The book of Ruth presents a lovely episode that occurred during the dark reign of the judges. Ruth, a Moabitess, married an Israelite man, who later died. Ruth decided to follow her mother-in-law, Naomi, back to the Promised Land, where she learned to know and serve the true God. She then fell in love and married Boaz, a relative of her deceased husband. One of their children was the grandfather of King David, making Ruth one of the ancestors of Jesus Christ of Nazareth, the promised Messiah.

Grace of God

The book not only gives us certain links in the ancestry of David and Jesus; it is also a wonderful demonstration of God's grace reaching down to a Gentile (non-Jewish) woman, who, after learning about the true God, became a spiritual Jew and a part of the Messiah's human ancestry.

First Samuel

First Samuel follows chronologically after the book of Judges. It opens by describing Eli, the last of the judges, and the birth of Samuel the prophet. The continual sin of Israel made it necessary for God to call Samuel, the first of the Great Prophets. The book tells of the circumstances surrounding the birth of Samuel and how, as a young child, he was dedicated to the Lord.

The book describes the ungodly sons of Eli and their sins against God, which led to the capture of the Ark of the Covenant by the raiding Philistines (1-6). The Lord caused the Philistines to bring back the Ark (7) and Samuel, the man of God, ruled the people.

The First King

The people, however, were not satisfied and rebelliously asked the Lord for a king. God gave them a king named Saul, according to their desire (8-12). He was not God's choice. Saul achieved victories over his enemies, but in his own strength, not the Lord's, and was a constant problem to the Lord (13-15).

David Chosen

God then commissioned Samuel to anoint "a man after His own heart" to be king. That man was David. That development led to jealousy on the part of Saul, who repeatedly tried to kill David. David was forced to flee and to hide out as a fugitive as long as Saul was alive (19-27). Saul eventually died in a battle with the Philistines, opening the way for David, the divinely chosen king, to reign in Israel. The first book of Samuel closes with Saul's death.

Second Samuel

Second Samuel relates the history of the reign of King David. After Saul's

The smoking crater of Mount Aetna. A weak illustration of 2 Peter 3:10: "But the day of the Lord will come like a thief, in which the heavens will pass away with a roar and the elements will be destroyed with intense heat, and the earth and its works will be burned up."

death, David was proclaimed king over the tribe of Judah in the city of Hebron (1-2). One of the generals of the deceased king placed one of Saul's sons on the throne of all Israel. Although David attempted to achieve a peaceful settlement with that son, his efforts failed because of the plots of others.

David's Reign

Finally, David ascended to the throne as king over all the Israelite people. He made Jerusalem his residence and brought the Ark of the Covenant there. David wanted to build a temple in Jerusalem to the Lord, but because he was a warrior and not a man of peace, God would not permit him to do that (5-7). This job was to be accomplished by David's son Solomon. During his reign, David defeated his enemies and established Israel as a mighty nation (8-10).

David's Sin

Yet he fell into the sins of adultery and murder (11-12), for which God punished him severly: his family was torn with strife and feuding, his illegitimate child by Bathsheba died, and his eldest son Amnon was murdered by his brother Absalom (12-13). David banished Absalom from his kingdom, but Absalom led an insurrection and proclaimed himself king, forcing David again to flee. David amassed an army and retook his kingdom, but his son Absalom died in the battle. The death of Absalom broke David's heart. He had truly loved his wayward son. David put down another uprising by a man named Sheba and settled an old feud between himself and the house of Saul (20-21). The book concludes with another failure of David, his prideful numbering of the people of Israel, which resulted in a plague brought upon them as God's judgment (24).

First Kings

The book of Kings, divided into 1 and 2 Kings in the English Bible, continues the story that was started in 2 Samuel. The two books of the Kings describe the monarchy from the death of David to its eventual fall. First Kings begins with the last days in the life of David, now an old man.

Solomon's Reign

After his death the kingdom went to his son Solomon, but not without an attempt by some people to make David's son Adonijah the king. Solomon followed his father's advice and made peace with various enemies, something his father had failed to do. God promised to grant Solomon any request, and Solomon chose to ask not for riches or fame, but rather for wisdom. God gave Solomon wisdom, but he also added riches, with which Solomon built a permanent temple to the Lord (5-8). God allowed Solomon's fame to increase, which caused the Queen of Sheba to come and admire his splendor and wisdom. Regrettably, Solomon did not obey God fully; he took many pagan wives, which led to his downfall. These women brought along their idols, and Solomon began to worship them. Therefore God removed the kingdom from him (11).

Kingdom Divided

A section from a drawing by Rembrandt: Jesus and the adulterous woman. Does Jesus write with His finger the curses of the law of Moses on the ground (Numbers 5:11-31), or does He consider how the hypocrisy of the bystanders can best be exposed (John 8)?

Solomon was succeeded by his son Rehoboam, under whom the kingdom was divided into two parts. Rehoboam reigned over two tribes, the southern kingdom of Judah (the tribes of Judah and Benjamin), while the ten northern tribes became subject to the reign of Jeroboam. First and Second Kings deal mainly with the history of the northern kingdom of Israel; the two books of Chronicles are concerned with the history of Judah.

Godless Kings of Israel; Elijah's Prophecies

First Kings centers on the dynasty of the godless kings Jeroboam (11-14) and Omri and Ahab (16-22). The people of the northern kingdom became deeply involved in idolatry and immorality, which led God to send the prophet Elijah to demonstrate in a miraculous way that the God of Israel was greater than the idols the people were worshiping (18). The many confrontations of Elijah with the evil king Ahab constitute the remainder of the book of Kings, with Ahab meeting his death in battle (22).

Second Kings

Second kings continues the account of the inglorious history of the northern kingdom. It begins by describing Elijah's ascension into heaven and his succession by the prophet Elisha. Elijah and Elisha were sent to bring the idolatrous northern kingdom back to God. Although they worked many miracles, the northern kingdom, as recorded in 2 Kings, included nine dynasties (some of only one king).

Collapse of Israel

Each new dynasty ascended to power by the murder of the previous king. For example, Ahab's house was destroyed by Jehu, who also incurred the wrath of the Lord because of his sins (9-15). Interspersed is information about the kings of the southern kingdom (1, 3, 8, 11, 12, 14, 16, 18-25). After the rapid succession of their kings, the northern kingdom came to an unceremonious end at the hand of the Assyrians. Many of the people were taken in exile to Assyria, and certain Assyrians were brought to Palestine to live. The Assyrians in Palestine intermarried with the Israelites

Jeremiah lamenting the fall of Jerusalem.

who were left behind: these became the Samaritans (17).

Collapse of Judah

The remainder of 2 Kings deals with the battles of the kingdom of Judah, first against the Assyrians (18-19) and then after the great revival under King Josiah, against King Nebuchadnezzar of Babylon (22-24). Jerusalem was eventually captured, and the city and magnificent temple were destroyed. The majority of the inhabitants of Judah (the Jews) went into exile in Babylon. Second Kings closes with the murder of Gedaliah, who had been appointed governor of those still living in Palestine, and with the elevation in Babylon of Jehoiachin, the former king of Judah.

First Chronicles

The books of Chronicles, like Samuel and Kings, are also divided into two books in our English Bible. First Chronicles begins by listing Israel's most important genealogies, going all the way back to Adam. It goes on the describe the history of King David and his descendants ruling in Jerusalem.

God's View

Chronicles, as opposed to Kings, gives God's view of history, showing

137

that this period was not one entirely of rebellion but had many positive aspects. Consequently, very little is said about the northern kingdom of Israel, or the sins of David, Solomon and the other kings. The things revealed point to the positive developments during this period. First Chronicles goes into detail about how the Ark of the Covenant was brought to Jerusalem (13-16), about the valiant deeds of David's mighty men (11-12, 18-20), and the preparations made by David for building the temple (17, 21-29).

Thus the book centers around God's work in Judah and Israel, represented by the kings in the line of David who obeyed the Lord's commandments.

Second Chronicles

Second Chronicles follows the pattern of 1 Chronicles, outlining the history of the kings of the house of David from Solomon to the exile. Emphasis is placed on how Solomon built the temple (2-8) rather than on the personal aspects of his life as described in 1 Kings.

Godly Kings

After Solomon, the emphasis is on the kings who obeyed the Lord and promoted worship of Him in the land. They include: Asa (14-16); Jehoshaphat (17-21); the reformation under the priest Jehoiada in the time of King Joash (22-24); Amaziah (25); the revival under Hezekiah (29-32); and the revival under Josiah (34-35). The sins of Judah, which led to the fall of Jerusalem and the Babylonian captivity, are mentioned only briefly. The book concludes with a proclamation by Cyrus ending the exile and the subsequent return of some of the Jewish people to Judah (36).

Ezra

Ezra begins with the words with which 2 Chronicles ends, the proclamation of King Cyrus that ended the exile. Ezra gives details about the religious and political restoration of the Jewish nation after the exile in Babylon. The first of the exiles returned under the leadership of Joshua and Zerubbabel (3). They courageously rebuilt the altar in Jerusalem, reintroduced the sacrifices, and celebrated the Feast of Tabernacles.

Rebuilding the Temple

They began rebuilding the temple even though there was opposition from their enemies. The work, in fact, had to be interrupted several times for fairly long periods (3-5). During that time the prophets Haggai and Zechariah encouraged the people to return to work on the temple. When the work was completed, the new temple was dedicated and the Passover was celebrated (5-6).

Influence of Ezra

Years later another group of exiles arrived in the land under the leadership of the scribe Ezra (7-8). Ezra called the people to follow the law of Moses. The people heeded the Word of God, confessed their sin and were restored to fellowship (9-10). The book of Ezra closes by describing how the people abandoned their ungodly practices.

Nehemiah

Nehemiah takes up the account where Ezra left off. Nehemiah, a cupbearer of King Artaxerxes of Persia, longed for the rebuilding of Jerusalem, its walls, and the altar and temple. The king gave his permission, and Nehemiah, despite intense opposition from the Samaritans, saw that this difficult work was carried out (1-7).

Renewal

The account reveals the faithfulness and trust that Nehemiah placed in God and the eventual reformation of the people under both Ezra and Nehemiah. Ezra publicly read the Law to the people, the Feast of Tabernacles was observed, and the covenant with God was renewed (8-10). The book lists the residents of Jerusalem, the priests and Levites, and describes

Even though the canonicity of the book of Esther had long been disputed, the book shows us in a marvelous way how God saves His people in spite of the judgment already determined by the alien powers. The prophet Zechariah (see picture) also prophesies about the redemption of the people of Israel. He sees the Lord moving out into battle against the gentile nations (Zechariah 14:1-7).

the dedication of the city walls (11-12).

Reformation

After a twelve-year absence Nehemiah returned to the land and instituted reforms. The people had strayed from the commandments of the Law. The book closes with Nehemiah's account of the reforms he made among the people (13).

Esther

The story of Esther is a story of the providence of God. God's people were in a strange land and were no longer visibly His people. Yet God protected them. This book is characterized by the total omission of God's name, but His care is evident. God's providence brought a young Jewish woman named Esther to the Persian court, where she was presented with an opportunity to save her people from destruction.

Jews Saved

A plot to destroy the Jews was made by an evil man named Haman, who was eventually hanged when his plot backfired. The Jews were allowed to avenge their enemies, and this victory was celebrated with the establishment of the Feast of Purim to be observed in commemoration of their being saved from total destruction.

Job

The book of Job has been called a literary masterpiece. The exact time of the events is incertain, but it probably took place around the time of Abraham, some 2,000 years before Christ.

Job's Loss

The account concerns a rich, God-fearing man named Job, who with God's permission was tested by Satan. Job lost everything he possessed, including his health, and he wished himself dead.

Three of his friends visited him and attempted to answer the profound question, "Why do the righteous suffer?" Although the book of Job never directly answers that question, it gives insight into the providence of God, who allows suffering in order to instruct His people. Only Job's young friend Elihu grasped something of this truth (32-37).

Restoration

But it was finally God Himself who answered Job (38-41). God's answer was, in effect, that if Job and his friends could not tell the methods God had used to create the physical universe, they had no right to asume that He was unjust to allow a part of that creation to suffer. Job then humbled himself for judging God for the events that had transpired, and God restored to Job much more than he had lost. Although the book of Job is very old, the universal problem it deals with faces people in all ages, making Job's story ever relevant.

Psalms

The book of Psalms is a collection of 150 songs, prayers and instructions. In the Psalms the full range of human emotions, such as pain, joy, fear, hope and trust, are expressed to God. This book is helpful to believers of all ages. The Psalms can be divided into five sections.

In the first section (1-41) a faithful and righteous remnant of men and women put their hope and trust in the Messiah—described variously as the Son of God (2), the Son of Man (8), the Lowly One (16), the Suffering and Glorified Servant (22) and the True Sacrifice (40).

Suffering

The next section (42-72) deals with the suffering of the faithful and of the Messiah (69). It also shows the Messiah's final glorification and reign (72).

History

The third section (73-89) reflects the history from the beginning of the 12 tribes of Israel.

Messiah's Reign

The fourth section (90-106) deals with the reign of the Lord that would be established by the Messiah after His suffering (102). The section also points to the ultimate salvation of God's people in accordance with the promises He made to the patriarchs (105-106).

Restoration

The fifth section (107-150) gives more details about the Messiah and the restoration of God's people. The ascent to Jerusalem is covered in the

Songs of Ascent (120-134), and the book closes with magnificent anthems of praise to the Lord God.

Proverbs

The book of Proverbs is a collection of short wise sayings on a variety of subjects dealing with human experience. The proverbs emphasize external religious life, teaching individuals how to live and overcome daily temptation. The Proverbs express a belief in God who is ruling over the universe; they seek to make the religion He has revealed become the controlling motive in everyday life and conduct.

"Then a shoot will spring from the stem of Jesus, and a branch from his roots will bear fruit. And the Spirit of the Lord will rest on Him, the Spirit of wisdom and understanding, the spirit of counsel and strength, the spirit of knowledge and the fear of the Lord, and He will delight in the fear of the Lord" (Isaiah 11,1-3a).

Ecclesiastes

The book of Ecclesiastes is the attempt of a wise man (Solomon) to find the meaning of life and true happiness *apart* from divine revelation. He has a limited perspective, and consequently he sees everything as senseless and hopeless. This pessimistic book shows the futility of trying to live one's life apart from God. No matter how wise a person may be, he or she will not find lasting meaning apart from divine revelation. Wisdom without God is foolishness. Only God gives meaning to life.

The Song of Solomon

The Song of Solomon is a collection of beautiful love songs from King Solomon, the bridegroom-shepherd, and his Shulammite bride. The book is more than a collection of love songs, however. It can also be seen as typifying the love between God and His people. Thus, spiritual truths can be gained from reading and applying its insights to one's own life.

Isaiah

The book of Isaiah has a wide scope. Isaiah prophesied from around 720 to 675 B.C.

Warnings, and Promises of the Messiah

He began by warning the people of the fall of Judah and Jerusalem and the coming judgments. Yet there is also a promise of restoration under the Messiah (1-4). Isaiah then records a sevenfold "woe" against the people, comparing them to a vineyard that had disappointed God. There is also a woe directed at Isaiah, who is shown to be just as sinful as any other man (5-6). Next comes the prophecy about the virgin birth of the coming Messiah. He would be the hope of those who were faithful to God. Though judgment was imminent, the Messiah would someday establish His kingdom (7-9). Isaiah then talks about the previous warnings the nation had received and about their greatest threat, the Assyrians, The Messiah would conquer their enemies and establish His glorious kingdom of peace (9-12).

Exile and Restoration

The second part of the book (13-27) announces judgement against the surrounding nations, especially Israel's new enemy, Babylon. The exile of Israel is prophesized, but also a future restoration. A future resurrection is predicted for God's people (24-27).

Redemption

The third main section (28-35) prophesies the attacks of different nations against the people of God. Spiritual lessons are drawn and applied to Israel who, according to these prophecies, eventually would become a redeemed people enjoying the full blessing of God.

History

The next section (36-39) is purely historical, but is vital for understanding the different prophecies.

The Future

The last main section (40-66) concerns God's preparation for the certain deliverance of His people. They will be restored and the Messianic kingdom will be set up (58-66).

Jeremiah

The book of Jeremiah chronicles the long history of the prophet Jeremiah and the courageous prophecies he uttered against successive kings of Judah. Jeremiah witnessed the fall of Jerusalem, which was followed by his forced departure for Egypt with part of the defeated nation.

Jeremiah's Life

His entire life consisted of a series of admonitions to Judah; he kept prophesying the imminent judgment that would strike the people because of their sin. The judgment, to be carried out by the Babylonians, could no longer be postponed. Zedekiah, the final king, was told repeatedly to turn the city over to those besieging it; his refusal finally led to his fall and the city's total devastation. The book is punctuated by distressing episodes in the life of Jeremiah (7, 11, 13, 18-22, 26-29, 32-44).

Prophecies

The book also contains messianic prophecies about the restoration of the repentant people (3), about the "Branch" from the line of David (23), and about God's everlasting love for the 12 tribes. It tells of Israel's restoration under the Son of David, the new covenant made with the people in the end-time, and their blessed future in a restored land and a restored city (30-33).

Fall of Jerusalem

After that, the book describes the history of Zedekiah, the fall of Jerusalem, and the flight into Egypt (where the people were still practicing idolatry). It closes by pronouncing judgment on a number of nations, including Babylon (46-51). Chapter 52 is a historical appendix.

Lamentations

The book of Lamentations contains Jeremiah's words of grief over the destruction of Jerusalem and the captivity of God's chosen people.

Tragedy

It was a terrible thing that God had to destroy the city He had chosen for His people, along with the temple and the altar. Jeremiah recognized that God's justice could not do otherwise since the people had sinned grievously against Him.

Hope

Yet as always there was the hope and assurance that someday all that was destroyed would be restored to those who repented and turned to the Lord.

Ezekiel

The book of Ezekiel was written by a prophet who was also a priest in Jerusalem. He was among the first to be deported to Babylon, where the people settled by the river Chebar. It was there that Ezekiel prophesied for over 20 years to those in exile, both before and after the fall of Jerusalem under Zedekiah. Ezekiel did in Babylon what Jeremiah had done in Jerusalem. He pointed out to the people that the judgments that fell upon them were a result of their sins.

Prophesies

The first section (1-24) contains prophesies that date before the fall of Jerusalem, starting with Ezekiel's vision of the glory of the Lord, followed by the devastation of the city and land. Ezekiel also sees the idolatry being committed in the temple itself and the subsequent departure of the glory of the Lord from the temple and the city (1-11).

Admonitions

Ezekiel sternly admonishes the leaders and false prophets, and warns about the city and successive kings of Judah (12-19). The prophet emphasizes that Judah had placed itself in the same position as the ten tribes of the nothern kingdom and would therefore meet the same fate (20-24). Though Judah was to be judged, the surrounding nations were also to experience the wrath of the Lord, with God using as His instrument King Nebuchadnezzar of Babylon (25-32).

Promises

Next comes a series of messianic predictions (33-39) announcing the true Shepherd, the Messiah, the Son of David. Ezekiel prophesies the devastation of Edom, an archenemy of Israel. There is also the prediction of a future restoration of Israel where the 12 tribes will again be united, and their enemies, Gog and Magog, will be destroyed. The final part of the book (40-48) describes the new temple, which will function when order is restored in the land.

Daniel

The book of Daniel deals with the history of the Jews as captives of the Babylonians and the Persians.

World Empires

It also deals with the destiny of four successive world kingdoms that would arise. Daniel lived at the time of two of these kingdoms, the Babylonian empire and the empire of the Medes and Persians. He also prophesied about the coming Greek and Roman empires. Because of the wisdom God gave him, he was kept at the Babylonian court by successive rulers as an advisor and even as a government official. But all the time he kept himself faithful to the one true God. The four world empires were first introduced in the form of a huge statue shown to King Nebuchadnezzar in a dream. The last empire would be destroyed by the Messiah at His coming. Daniel also saw the four empires in a dream, but he saw them in their true character, as four beasts.

Seventy Weeks

Interwoven with the history of those kingdoms is the history of rejected Israel, which hoped for restoration. That hope was confirmed to them by the prophecy of the "Seventy Weeks," which concerned Israel and Jerusalem and foretold the Messiah's future reign. The book closes with a prediction of the nation's restoration.

Hosea

Hosea is the first of the so-called Minor Prophets. They are designated such, not because their message was inferior to the Major Prophets but because of the size of their books. Hosea records the rejection of both the northern kingdom of Israel and the southern kingdom of Judah. Israel would be left without a king, without their unique relationship with God, until the last days when they again come to acknowledge both the Lord and His Messiah. At that time Israel will be converted and restored with the blessings of the Lord.

Joel

The book of Joel predicts the destruction of the Assyrian army by means of a famine bound up with the Day of the Lord, the coming time when the enemies of God would be destroyed. A remnant of God's people would be converted and God's Spirit would be poured out upon all who were His own. In the end all the nations would be judged and God's people would receive His blessings.

Amos

The book of Amos pronounces judgment on the surrounding nations because of their sins. At the same time the prophet Amos also declares that the longsuffering God will not bear with Israel's own unrighteousness any longer. Judgment will come to them as well. As always predicted, however, a righteous remnant will be preserved and blessed under the Messiah.

Obadiah

Obadiah is a prophecy against Edom, a brother nation of Israel known for its jealously and hatred of the people of God. Obadiah's prophecy is extended to all the nations and points ahead to the Day of the Lord when the Messiah will judge the earth and redeem Zion, the Holy Mountain of Jerusalem.

Jonah

The book of Jonah demonstrates that even though the Lord had chosen Israel to be His people, His care and concern extended to all humankind. Jonah was sent to the godless Assyrains to pronounce judgment on the capital city, Nineveh. After running away from his calling and being swallowed by a large fish, Jonah, miraculously still alive, was able to proceed to fulfill his mission.

Repentance

Although the message was one of doom, the people of Nineveh repented, throwing themselves on the mercy of God, who decided to spare their city. The message of the book teaches that God's grace extends to everyone, whether Jew or Gentile.

Micah

Micah, a younger contemporary of the prophet Isaiah, pronounces judgment from God on both Israel and Judah. The land had been so thoroughly polluted with their sin that it could no longer be a haven for godly people. God, through Micah, denounced the leaders and the false prophets in Jerusalem, predicting their destruction. Micah proclaimed that the city would be restored in the last days, but before that would occur, Jerusalem would be destroyed and the people would be scattered.

Deliverance

Micah also predicted that the Messiah would someday come, deliver His people, bless them, and rule over them. All unrighteousness would be removed. After those predictions, Micah again warned the people against serving idols. He laments the sinful condition of the people, but at the same time looks for the fulfillment of God's promises.

Nahum

Nahum predicts the destruction of one of Israel's enemies, the people of Nineveh (the Assryians). Nineveh not only would be destroyed — it would never be restored. The Assyrians, who had troubled God's people for a long time, were regarded as the most brutal of all ancient heathen nations, and Nahum prophesied God's vengeance on them for their terrible acts. Nahum reminds his readers that wickedness will be judged, but the righteous will be saved. God is the sovereign ruler in all human affairs.

Habakkuk

Habakkuk, another prophet of God, relates some of his personal experiences. He was troubled by the unrighteousness of God's people, wondering why their sins were going unpunished. God showed him that He did intend to punish the people for their sins: He would send the Babylonians against them. Consequently, Habakkuk took pity on the people and asked the Lord to be merciful.

God's Reassurances

He then brought before the Lord accusations against the sinful Babylonians, God's intended instrument of judgment. God told Habukkuk that the Babylonians would also be punished, but that meanwhile the righteous would live by faith. The Day of the Lord was coming and all the earth would be filled with the knowledge of His glory. The book ends with Habakkuk rejoicing at recalling God's earlier deliverances and looking forward to the glorious future.

Zephaniah

The prophet Zephaniah announces imminent judgment on the land because of unrighteousness, hypocrisy and idolatry. This day of judgment, the Day of the Lord, would also come upon the surrounding nations. Zephaniah also spoke of a remnant of people in Jerusalem who had trusted in the Lord; he called on these faithful men and women to watch and wait. The destiny of these people was connected with the end times.

Gentile Belivers

Zephaniah foresaw believers coming from the Gentile nations, along with a spiritual and natural restoration for Israel. God's love for His people would be made manifest, making Israel renowned among all the peoples of the earth.

Haggai

Haggai is the first of the three prophetic books written after the exile. This prophet was one of the men who had encouraged the people to finish rebuilding the temple. After the temple was completed, Haggai declared that God would be with His people with His Word and Spirit and that He would one day shake the heavens and the earth. At that time the Gentiles would turn to the Messiah, and the temple would be filled with the glory of the Lord.

Zechariah

The book of Zechariah can be divided into two sections.

Destiny of Jerusalem

The first section (1-6) contains eight visions dealing with the destiny of Jerusalem. Jerusalem was at the mercy of four successive world empires (introduced as "horns" and "chariots," 1-6). Zechariah foresaw judgment for those nations along with a restoration of the city to its former splendor under the Messiah, the "Branch" (3, 6).

The Messiah

The second section contains three "words of the Lord," again with Jerusalem and the Messiah as the theme. The first division (7-8) describes Jerusalem's future restoration under the Messiah. The second subdivision (9-11) introduces the same Messiah in the lowly estate that He would assume at the time of His first coming. After His rejection, Israel would be delivered into the hands of a "worthless shepherd."

Second Coming

The last of the three words of God (12-14) speaks of the redemption of Jerusalem at the time of the Second Coming of the Messiah, along with the conversion and reconciliation of the faithful. The book closes by prophesying the glorious final destiny of the city and its inhabitants.

Malachi

Malachi, the last book of the Old Testament, describes the great moral decline of the Jewish people after their return from the Babylonian captivity. Despite God's unfailing love toward them, the people had forsaken His commandments. This caused Malachi to rebuke sharply their unholiness, faithless sacrifices and unworthy priests.

Forerunners and the Messiah

Malachi predicted the coming of a forerunner of the Messiah (fulfilled in John the Baptist). A prediction follows, about the coming of the Messiah, who would sift the people in judgment, sparing the faithful ones. The Old Testament here concludes with references to two of its greatest figures, Moses and Elijah. There is a call to return to the Law of Moses and an announcement about the prophet Elijah, who will come before the Day of the Lord.

CHAPTER NINE

The Contents of the New Testament

Someone said concerning the two Testaments, "The New is in the Old contained; the Old is in the New explained." The Old Testament presents the promises and the Law. The New Testament presents Jesus Christ as fulfilling the Old Testament Law and promises. From the beginning the Old Testament predicted the coming Messiah who would save His people from their sins.

The following chart lists the books of the New Testament in the order given in the English Bible. As was true with the Old Testament chart, the dates are approximate.

Book	Author	Approximate Date of Compositiion A.D.
Matthew	Matthew	50-70
Mark	Mark	50-70
Luke	Luke	60
John	John	60-95
Acts	Luke	63
Romans	Paul	57
1 Corinthians	Paul	56
2 Corinthians	Paul	57
Galatians	Paul	50
Ephesians	Paul	62
Philippians	Paul	62
Colossians	Paul	62
1 Thessalonians	Paul	50
2 Thessalonians	Paul	51
1 Timothy	Paul	63
2 Timothy	Paul	63
Titus	Paul	63
Philemon	Paul	62
Hebrews	Unknown	68
James	James	55
1 Peter	Peter	62
2 Peter	Peter	65
1 John	John	60-95
2 John	John	60-95
3 John	John	60-95
Jude	Jude	65-80
Revelation	John	60-95

Page 148: When Isaiah's prophecy was fulfilled (see page 147), Jesus preached on the banks of the Sea of Galilee, calling to His disciples: "Follow Me, and I will make you fishers of men" (Matthew 4:18-20).

Matthew

The Gospel According to Matthew, the first book of the New Testament, sees Jesus Christ as King of the Jews, the one who fulfilled the Old Testament prophecies about the Messiah.

Transition

In charting Jesus' ministry, Matthew regards Jesus' miracles as a sign that He was indeed the long-awaited Messiah. But the people rejected both Him and His testimony. Still, Jesus talked about building His church, which would consist of both Jews and Gentiles. Thus, Matthew's gospel is a fitting transition between the Old and New Testaments.

Jesus washing His disciples' feet. "I say to you, a slave is not greater than his master; neither is one who is sent greater than the one who sent him" (John 13:16,17).

Matthew began his book by linking Jesus with David the king and with Abraham, the father of the faithful. He gave an account of the birth of Jesus, conceived by the Holy Spirit and born of the virgin Mary. He was *Immanuel,* "God with us." Writing of Jesus' genealogy, birth and the preparations for His ministry, Matthew consistently emphasized that prophecy was being fulfilled (1:1 – 4:11).

Ministry

After that came Jesus' work in northern Galilee, where He delivered the Sermon on the Mount to expound the principles of the kingdom of heaven (4:12 – 7:29). Jesus sent out His disciples, who were given ability to perform miracles (8-10). Then followed the rejection of Jesus' forerunner, John the Baptist, and soon of Jesus Himself (11-12). Jesus told seven parables pointing out the future character of the unified kingdom of heaven (13). His ministry would extend beyond Israel, as Savior of the world.

Death and Resurrection

Jesus began to predict His suffering, atoning death and resurrection (14-18). He concluded His teaching ministry in Judea and entered Jerusalem (19-22). Matthew's gospel concludes with an account of Jesus'

150

betrayal, death, resurrection and His commission to His disciples to preach the gospel to all the world (28).

Mark

The Gospel According to Mark is the shortest of the four gospels, giving a straightforward account of the ministry of Jesus Christ.

Servant

Mark portrays Jesus as both the Servant of the Lord and the Son of God. His emphasis is not so much on the statements and discourses of Jesus, as on the work He accomplished as the Servant of the Lord.

After a brief introduction, Mark describes Jesus' ministry in Galilee, where He performed seven miracles of healing. Christ taught about hidden principles of the kingdom of God and showed signs of His power and authority (1:14 — 5:43).

Rejection

During further travels in Galilee He encountered sinful conditions and people who rejected His ministry. Jesus prophesied His future suffering (6-9). He continued to minister to people on the way to Judea, in Jericho, and finally in Jerusalem (10-13). He was crucified in Jerusalem, yet three days later He rose from the dead. The book closes with the resurrected Jesus Christ in Galilee, commissioning His disciples to preach the gospel to everyone.

Luke

The Gospel According to Luke presents Jesus as the perfect man. Jesus designated Himself the Son of Man, the man from God for all humanity, the Savior of the entire world.

Humanity

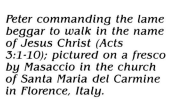

Peter commanding the lame beggar to walk in the name of Jesus Christ (Acts 3:1-10); pictured on a fresco by Masaccio in the church of Santa Maria del Carmine in Florence, Italy.

Luke's account stresses His humanity, giving details of His birth and boyhood (1-2). He describes Jesus' preparation for His ministry, His baptism and His temptation (3:1 — 4:13). Next came His work in Galilee (4:19 — 9:50), which included the calling of His disciples. Jesus explained His task and purpose, and predicted His sufffering. Luke gives detailed descriptions of happenings on the way to Jerusalem (9:51 — 19:28). He records events in Samaria, Jesus' conversations with the Pharisees, and His miraculous healings.

Betrayal

The closing part (19:24 — 24:53) covers Jesus' entry into Jerusalem, the conflicts He faced, the last supper, His betrayal, arrest, trials, crucifixion, burial, resurrection, appearances, commissioning of His disciples and ascension.

John

The Gospel According to John was the last of the four gospels to be written. It shows, by inference, acquaintance with the other three. John presents Jesus as God in human flesh. He is the one who was in the beginning, the creator of all things. John's purpose in writing this Gospel is

151

to reveal Jesus as God's Son, the one who gives life to everyone who believes (20:31)

In the prologue (1:1-18) Jesus is presented as the eternal Word who became flesh. Later He is depicted as the Lamb of God, the One who will take away the sin of the world (1:29). John records Jesus' first miracle, turning water into wine at a wedding in Cana (2). He reports the conversation between Jesus and Nicodemus, a religious ruler. Nicodemus was told that he had to be "born again" (3). Afterward Jesus went to Samaria, where He talked with a Samaritan woman about the true worship of God (4). In the next section (5-7) Jesus explained more about who He was:

The promise of Jesus by the Sea of Galilee has been fulfilled: the disciples became fishers of men. That is how this book, being read at this very moment, came to be written almost two thousand years later.

the Son of God who gives life (5), the Son of Man who lays down His life (6) and the one who later will be glorified (7).

Light of the World

The next main section (8-12) pictures Christ as the light of the world, but rejected in His person, words (8), and works (9). John also describes Him as the Good Shepherd who lays down His life for His sheep (10). Jesus showed His power by raising Lazarus from the dead (11). Still rejected by the Jews, He began talking about His coming death (12). That ended His public witness; from then on He is seen in the midst of His disciples.

With Disciples

The next section (13-17) shows Jesus in the upper room where He celebrated the Passover. He washed the feet of His disciples and predicted His death on the cross (13). About to return to the Father and to send the Holy Spirit as the Comforter, Jesus explained the disciples' future position (14-16). He prayed, asking the Father to glorify the Son and in the future to bless and strengthen all believers (17).

Arrest

Then John told the passion story: the arrest of Christ, His appearance before Anna, Caiaphas, and Pilate; His crucifixion, burial, resurrection and appearances at the Sea of Galilee (18-21).

The Acts of the Apostles

The Acts of the Apostles is a direct continuation of Luke's gospel, giving the history of the early church in Palestine, Asia Minor and Europe. The book is basically limited to the ministries of Peter and Paul and, because of the prominence given to Paul's travels, it provides significant background for understanding Paul's epistles.

Church Growth

After a foreword, where Luke connects Acts with his gospel, he repeats the account of Christ's ascension. While the disciples waited for the outpouring of the Holy Spirit, they appointed a replacement for Judas (1). At Pentecost, 50 days after the resurrection, the Holy Spirit descended, authenticating the New Testament manifestation of the church. The power of the Holy Spirit became evident through the disciples, and the church grew quickly despite intense opposition (2-5). Persecution set in with the martyrdom of Stephen (6-7). The gospel reached Samaria and an Ethiopian eunuch (8). Saul of Tarsus was converted and became the apostle Paul (9). The gospel also went to the Gentiles (10) and continued to spread throughout pagan lands (11-12).

Paul

The next section contains the three missionary journeys of Paul. During the first journey (13:1 — 15:39) Paul ministered in Cyprus, in Pisidia (Asia Minor) and in the Galatian cities of Iconium, Lystra, and Derba. He returned to Antioch. Then followed the council at Jerusalem, where the relationship of Christian believers to the Jewish Law was discussed. On his second journey (15:40 — 18:22) Paul revisited Derbe and Lystra, traveled through Asia Minor to Troas, and crossed over to Europe. He ministered in Philippi, Thessalonica, Berea, Athens, Corinth and made a brief visit to Palestine and Antioch.

Many places to which Paul had addressed his epistles are no longer in existence or else in ruins. Philippi—today a field of ruins—is dominated by the high pillars of a 6th century basilica. This building seems never to have been completed, because the cupola fell in while it was being erected.

On his third journey (18:23 — 21:16) Paul passed through Galatia and Phrygia, spending a long time in Ephesus, where he encountered much opposition. He crossed over to Macedonia and journeyed to Greece. After staying in Corinth, where he probably wrote the book of Romans, he returned to Macedonia. He crossed over to Troas, where Eutychus was raised from the dead. Paul bade farewell to the elders at Ephesus on the coast by Miletus, crossed over to Tyre and went to Jerusalem via Caesarea.

He was arrested in Jerusalem and appeared before the Sanhedrin, before the governors Felix and Festus, and before King Agrippa. He was then taken to Rome as a prisoner, where he wrote the books of Philemon, Ephesians, Colossians, and Philippians. The book of Acts ends with Paul's stay and preaching in Rome.

Romans

The epistle to the Romans is addressed to a church that was not founded by Paul. He had never been in Rome, although he longed to visit the believers there (1:13; 15:22-23). He wrote the letter because he wanted to take the gospel to the Roman believers (1:15) and because he wished to announce his planned stopover in Rome on a journey to Spain (15:24-29).

Teachings

After the introduction, Paul, in a long doctrinal section, shows how humanity has by nature failed God. Human beings have no righteousness (ability to be right in God's eyes) except through faith in the work of Christ. That is the only basis through which anyone can know God and find forgiveness of sin. Paul illustrates that truth by giving the example of Abraham, who was considered righteous apart from the Law—that is, by faith alone. Abraham believed that God could indeed bring life out of death (as He has proven in the resurrection of Jesus Christ) (3:21-4:25). Great blessings are attached to "justification by faith": Not only are a believer's sins forgiven, but that person is also saved from the

The apostle Paul preaching, pictured on a tapestry after a design by Audran, 17th century (Mobilier National, Paris). "For since in the wisdom of God the world through its wisdom did not come to know God, God was well-pleased through the foolishness of the message preached to save those who believe" (1 Corinthians 1:21).

power of sin. Hence, believers no longer belong to the family of Adam, but to the family of Christ (5).

Paul applied this freedom to practical areas of life. Because believers died with Christ on the cross, sin no longer rules over them. Its power has been broken. They have become bondservants of God (6), no longer under the yoke of the Law (7). Consequently, believers can live for Christ by the power of the Spirit and have a glorious hope for the future (8).

Israel

In the second main section (9-11) Paul deals with the special position of Israel. Although Israel has been set aside temporarily there will be full reinstatement in the future.

Exhortations

The third section (12-16) includes admonitions about the believer's attitude toward God, neighbors, those in authority (13), and the weak in faith who do not fully understand Christian liberty (14-15). The epistle closes with many greetings along with final exhortations and a beautiful doxology (15-16).

First Corinthians

First Corinthians is the apostle Paul's response to a letter brought to him that detailed some of the problems in the church of Corinth.

Rebuke

After expressing thankfulness, Paul discusses the abuses reported to him: a spirit of contentiousness and the rise of factions. He contrasts such attitudes with the "foolishness of the cross" and the true character of Christian service, pointing to himself as an example (1-4). Immorality had been condoned within the church (5-6), and pagan courts were used to settle quarrels between Christians (6). Paul rebukes both of those practices.

Some say that Paul was ill disposed to women, since he himself was not married. And yet, he compares marriage and the relationship between husband and wife with that of Christ and His Church (Ephesians 5:22-33).

Questions

In the next section Paul deals with questions the Corinthians had asked about marriage and celibacy (7); eating meat that had been offered to idols (which issue the apostle then incorporates into an important explanation of the communion service) (8-10); the question of the gifts of the Spirit and their orderly use in church meetings (12-14); and the question of the resurrection, on which the entire Christian faith is based (15). Paul concludes with practical advice, admonitions and greetings (16).

Second Corinthians

The occasion of 2 Corinthians was a meeting in Macedonia between Paul and Titus. Titus had brought good news from Corinth, which led Paul to write another letter to that church. Second Corinthians begins with the customary greeting and thanksgiving for the comfort Paul had received during his recent persecution and affliction.

Defense of Ministry

Then follows the main section of the letter (1:12 — 7:16) in which Paul, in detail, defends his apostolic ministry. He reveals the purpose in changing his plans and the nature of his ministry (3-7). He is the minister of the New Covenant, which fulfills the Old Covenant under the law of Moses (3). That ministry consists of administering an immense treasure, although the ministers themselves are but "earthen vessels" (4). This ministry is carried out in light of the judgment seat of Christ, and contains God's offer of reconciliation based on Jesus Christ's death on the cross (5). Paul carried out this ministry in much affliction and prays that the Corinthians would also walk the straight and narrow path (6). Then follows a report on his meeting with Titus (7). In the next section (8-9) Paul reveals the necessity of collecting money for the poor in Judea.

Defense of Self

In the last section (10-13) he gives a personal defense of himself as an apostle against those who challenged his authority (10). Paul refutes their arguments and shows that Christ considered his apostleship important in that He allowed Paul to suffer so much (11). The apostle reveals some of the unique revelations he has received from God (12). He closes with remarks about his planned visit with them, pronouncing his well-known benediction (12-13).

Galatians

The letter to the Galatians is a strong protest by Paul against the influence of certain Judaizers who were undermining the churches by attempting to rob them of their freedom in Christ. These Judaizers were trying to impose the law of Moses, including circumcision, on the people. They also sought to discredit Paul's apostleship. The letter can be divided into three parts: historical (1-2), doctrinal (3-4) and practical (5-6).

Paul's Call

Paul begins with an emphatic assertion that he has been called by God to be an apostle. He goes on to condemn those who would undermine the gospel. He himself had once fought for the traditionns of the fathers, yet God called him to preach the gospel to the Gentiles. The other apostles confirmed this calling. Paul even had to rebuke Peter for being inconsistent in the matter of the law and Christian liberty.

Law Versus Faith

In the next section, the apostle explains in greater detail why a legalistic Christianity is wrong. The Galatians had become believers not through the law, but through faith in Christ. Paul reminds them that the blessings received by Abraham did not come to him through the law, but through faith. The law can bring only condemnation for sinners, but Christ freed believers from condemnation by becoming a curse in their stead. Similarly, the law did not cancel the promise given earlier, but was added to it as a "tutor" to convict humanity of sinfulness and to point them to the coming Christ. Now that Christ had come, "infancy" under the law was to give way to liberty and to responsiblity in sonship. Paul illustrates this idea by an allegorical application of the Old Testament story of Sarah, Hagar and their sons.

Liberty

In his concluding section Paul makes clear that Christian freedom excludes circumcision and other ritualistic practices of Judaism. At the same

156

time he shows that liberty of the Spirit is not the same as liberty of the flesh (our sinful nature). Spiritual liberty in Christ makes one compassionate and gives him a desire to reach out to others. In his epilogue, Paul underscores the importance of this letter, written with his own hand. He contrasts the false motives of the Judaizers with his boasting solely in the cross of Christ. The letter closes with a general greeting.

Ephesians

The letter to the Ephesians is a profound treatise by Paul dealing with the special position and privileges of the church in connection with its head, Jesus Christ.

"For our struggle is not against flesh and blood, but against the rulers, against the powers, against the world-forces of this darkness, against the spiritual forces of wickedness in the heavenly places." This is written by Paul to the church at Ephesus (Ephesians 6:12). Not only is Paul said to have written to the church at Ephesus, but probably John also wrote his epistles from Ephesus. This unearthed basilica is said to have been built over John's grave.

Spiritual Blessings

The letter begins with words of praise to God who has blessed His children with all spiritual blessings in Christ Jesus. Believers possess these blessings because they are the chosen ones, redeemed by the blood of Christ. They have become joint heirs with Him, having received the Holy Spirit as a "down payment" of their inheritance. Paul prayed that his readers would be granted wisdom to understand the riches of this revelation. He also prayed that they would grasp the power by which God raised Christ from the dead. By that same power He has raised them up spiritually and seated them in the heavenly realm. This is the believer's position in Christ (1:1-2:10).

One Body

Paul then goes on to mention the collective blessings of Christ's sacrifice. The Gentiles, who formerly were strangers to the news of the covenant and the promises, have now been joined in one church, one body, with the spiritual Jews. Similarly, the Jews, formerly separated from other nations by the Law, are now one in Christ with the believing Gentiles. That revelation, which had not been fully understood in former ages, now had been revealed, and Paul here sheds light on God's plan for the church.

157

This truth led Paul to another prayer. He asked Christ to dwell in the hearts of believers (2:11-3:21).

Applications

The second part of the letter (4-6) is a practical application of these teachings, dealing with maintaining unity, the different gifts within the church, and the old and new life as worked out in the lives of believers, in marriage, in the family and in the vocational sphere. These truths are to be implemented in people's lives. The letter closes with practical remarks and a benediction.

Philippians

The letter to the Philippians is Paul's warm reply to the love expressed to him by the church of Philippi during his Roman imprisonment. Epaphroditus, the one who had brought their gifts to Paul, had been very ill, but had recovered. Paul was now sending him back to Philippi with this letter (2:25-30).

Encouragments

After the opening greeting and words of thanksgiving for the Philippians' generosity and an assurance that he is praying for them, Paul describes his personal circumstances. He rejoices in his present situation, despite unfavorable news and uncertain prospects for his future. He encourages his readers to do likewise (1). He admonishes them to be of one mind and to display a humble, Christlike attitude. Paul then explains how Christ humbled himself on our behalf so that someday we could be exalted with Him. The apostle shows from his own example, along with the examples of Timothy and Epaphroditus, that such humility is indeed possible (2).

Warnings

Next he warns against the Judaizers. He contrasts pseudo-Christians, enemies of the cross, with the genuine citizens of heaven who are looking forward to Christ's second coming (3). In closing, Paul gives a general exhortation to the Philippians to be of one mind, to have joy and peace in the Lord and to keep their consciences pure. He repeats his appreciation for their generosity and sends final greetings (4).

Ephesus was, after Alexandria and Antioch, the biggest city in the East. The church here was founded by Paul during his third missionary journey.

Colossians

The occasion for Paul's letter to the Colossians was a report that dangerous heresies had gained a foothold in the church at Colossae. Those heresies, which included elements of Greek philosophy (asceticism) and Jewish ritual (circumcision, angel worship), were drawing believers away from Christ.

Praise

Paul opens with the usual thanksgiving and then records his prayer that the Colossians would walk in a manner worthy of the Lord, giving thanks to the Father who has richly blessed them in Christ. Paul then praises Christ as the Son of God's love, the creator of all things, the firstborn from the dead, the head of all things and especially the head of the body (the church). Christ laid the foundation for the reconciliation of all things. All wisdom and knowledge are in Christ, in whom dwells all the fullness of the Godhead and through whom believers also possess that fullness (1-2).

Application

The second part of the letter (3-4) applies these truths to practical matters of marriage, the family and society. The life of the believer is hidden with Christ in God. The letter closes with practical hints, greetings and messages, and a brief reference to Paul's own life.

First Thessalonians

First Thessalonians is Paul's answer to news brought by Timothy, his co-worker and traveling companion, from Thessalonica. Paul praises the Thessalonians for their perseverance, but also admonishes them for cer-

True religion fosters no discrimination between rich and poor and does not degenerate into dead orthodoxy, but rather, it expresses itself in good works which are the fruit of faith.

tain false teachings and misunderstandings, especially about the return of Christ.

Devotion

He begins by giving thanks for their testimony and devotion to God and for their eager expectation of Christ's return. Paul reminds them of the work he did among them and how they had received his word as the Word of God in spite of persecution. He describes how he longs for them and prays for their further growth (1-3).

Christ's Return

In the next part of the letter, Paul admonishes for purity in marriage, brotherly love and honest work. He then takes up the question of those who die before the return of the Lord. He assures the Thessalonians that those who die believing in Christ will be present when He returns. All believers, whether living or dead, will meet the Lord in the air when He comes for His church. Paul also explains that the time of Christ's return is not known. Christ's return will mean judgment for unbelievers. Christians will not be subject to judgment; nevertheless they must wait and be sober. The letter closes with practical admonitions and greetings.

Second Thessalonians

Paul sent his second letter to the Thessalonians shortly after his first in answer to a misconception on the part of the church in Thessalonica, namely, that the Day of the Lord had already come.

Judgment Day

The apostle begins by pointing out that although the believers had suffered persecution, this was not a sign that the judgment day had already come. It will be just the opposite when that day actually does come. Believers will be rewarded; oppressors will be condemned (1). Further, the Day of the Lord could not possibly have arrived yet, because it will be preceded by a falling away from the faith and the appearance of the Man of Sin (known also as the son of perdition, the man of lawlessness, or the Antichrist). Although the Antichrist will lead many astray, he will be destroyed by Christ at His coming (3).

The letter draws to a close with further thanksgiving and admonitions concerning prayer, ungodly living and disobedience. There is also a greeting written in Paul's own handwriting.

First Timothy

Paul's first letter to Timothy was probably written after his first imprisonment in Rome. He gives instructions to Timothy about his work in Ephesus, encouraging him to take a firm stand and not be ashamed of the gospel.

After the opening greeting and words of caution about the Ephesus situation, the apostle talks about his own experiences and reaffirms Timothy's commission (1).

Instructions

The next part of the letter (2-4) contains instructions about a variety of subjects including prayer, the position and attitude of women (2) and the qualifications of overseers and deacons. Paul then describes the church, the mystery of Christ's first coming and subsequent glorification (3) and certain threats to the church (4). He outlines correct church disciplinary procedure (5) and closes with various instructions about slaves, false teachers, the dangers of wealth, and Timothy's behavior as a "man of God."

Second Timothy

Paul's second letter to Timothy was written after he had been taken prisoner again, shortly before his martyrdom in Rome.

Encouragements

Looking back on what he had accomplished and ahead to his reward, Paul begins with his customary greetings and thanksgiving. He encourages Timothy by appealing to his gift of grace and the responsibility entrusted to him (1). Timothy is to persevere, the way good soldiers, champions and farmers have to persevere, keeping the final goal and reward in view. He must take a firm stand against false teachers and separate himself from all who continue to act unrighteously, identifying himself with those who call on the Lord from pure hearts (2). Paul then talks about the "Last Days," when the moral strength of Christianity fails in large measure (3).

Final Testimony

Then, knowing his death is imminent, Paul gives one last commission, one final testimony, several personal requests and a report on his defense before his judges. The letter closes with greetings and benedictions (4).

Titus

The letter to Titus is addressed to another fellow worker and spiritual son of the apostle Paul. On one missionary journey Paul had left Titus behind in Crete so that he could ordain elders in the churches and clear up certain problems that had resulted from the laziness of the Cretans and the influence of Jewish heretics. After reaffirming his own apostleship, Paul mentions the proper qualifications to be employed in choosing elders and then goes on to expose false teachers (1).

Christian Living

He speaks about the true Christian walk to which young and old are called, including men, women and slaves. This leads to a short summary of Christian doctrine (2). Finally the apostle writes about the proper attitude for Christians to take toward others. He reminds the Christians that they were once just like their sinful neighbors, but have been saved solely by the grace of God. The letter closes with practical admonitions, plans and greetings.

Philemon

The letter to Philemon was written after Paul became acquainted with Onesimus, a slave who had fled from his master, Philemon. After Onesimus came to know the Lord, Paul sent him back to his master in Colossae, who was already a believer and a friend of Paul.

Paul sent this letter with him to persuade Philemon to take back his runaway slave and to forgive him. Paul promised to reimburse Philemon for any financial loss he might have suffered because of Onesimus.

Hebrews

The letter to the Hebrews, whose author is unknown, was addressed to Jews and Jewish Christians who were familiar with the Old Testament as well as with the gospel. They were, however, still clinging to the Jewish law, worship services and nationalistic character of Jewish ceremonies.

These Jews were to give up this external, national brand of religion. It was useless to hold on to something that was a mere shadow of better things to come. Instead, they should trust the one who is the perfect fulfillment of the Old Testament sacrificial system.

Better Things

Hebrews, then, is a letter about "better things," beginning with the description of the glory of Jesus Christ, the Son of God. He is higher than the angels (1); as the Son of Man, He is higher than all creation (2); as the Son over the house of God, He is higher than Moses (3); as the one who leads His people into true rest, He is higher than Joshua (3-4); and as the high priest for His people, He is higher than Aaron (4-7). Christ instituted a complete covenant founded on better promises and based on His own sacrifice (8-10).

Look by Faith

Thus the Hebrews had to learn not to look to external things any longer, but to look by faith to the invisible, glorified Christ—just as the patriarchs had in essence lived by this faith. But the greatest example was Christ Himself. The Hebrews were to look to Him and to the better things He had initiated (11-12). That viewpoint is applied to practical circumstances. The letter closes with admonitions and greetings (13).

James

The book of James was written by the brother of Jesus who for a long time was leader of the Jerusalem church. It was addressed to Jewish Christians who were still connected with the synagogue (2:2) and who still clung to the Jewish law (1:25; 2:8) and customs (5-14).

The Believer's Attitude

James begins with a discourse on the meaning of trials and testing and the attitude a believer should take at such times. Readers are not only to hear his words, but also to do them (1). True religion fosters no discrimination between rich and poor and does not degenerate into dead orthodoxy. Rather, it expresses itself in good works which are the fruit of real faith (2). Teachers must be able to control their tongues and must show proper wisdom (3). Believers must guard against overestimation of self (4). In closing, the writer exposes the rich oppressors and points out the need for patience in times of trouble. James also talks about swearing falsely, interceding for the sick, and helping brothers and sisters who go astray or need help (5).

First Peter

The first letter of Peter is addressed to Jewish Christians who had believed in the Messiah. Peter points repeatedly to the example set by Christ during his life on earth. He describes the nature of salvation as the outcome of faith, the theme of the prophets and something to be worked out in a holy life (1:1 — 2:10).

Christians' Relationships

The next section (2:11-3:12) deals with relationships of Christians to the world, to the state, to their daily work, to their marriage partners, to other believers and to their calling in the world. The last chapter (5) describes the relationship between the elders and the "fold" and comments on the personal faithfulness of believers. Peter closes with practical details and greetings.

Second Peter

In the second letter of Peter, realizing his own death is near, the apostle warns believers against false teachers creeping into the churches.

True Knowledge

He cautions them against giving up the true knowledge which is a possession of all who are partakers of the divine nature. That knowledge has been confirmed by the eyewitness testimony of Peter and others who saw the life of Christ — and also through fulfilled prophecy. Peter warns against false knowledge that would come into the churches: God will uproot those false teachers, just as He has overthrown His enemies in the past. Peter explains the activities and dangers of false teachers and warns against those who scoff at Christ's return. God will destroy the godless in a flood of judgment that ushers in new heavens and a new earth. Believers are to walk in the light of that truth, growing and maturing in the grace and knowledge of God.

First John

First John was written to take issue with certain heresies that were undermining the truth about the person of Christ — namely, that He is truly God in human flesh.

John begins with testimony that the Son, who was eternally with the Father, lived visibly on earth in the form of flesh and blood. Believers have fellowship with the Son and the Father by possessing eternal life, which brings with it responsibilities.

Love is the Basis

Believers must recognize in their daily walk that God is light and that they must therefore obey His commandments and love others (1:5 — 2:11). John applies this to fathers, young men and children in the faith, warning of the spirit of Antichrist (2). The love of the Father is evident in that they have become children of God; this ought to be made visible in their obedience and love for all (3). Believers are to guard against false teachings about the person of Christ. They are to recognize that God is love, which He demonstrated by sending His Son (4). God's love gives believers security and a basis for obedience (5).

Second John

Second John is addressed to an "elect lady" and her children. Similar in character to 1 John, its key word is *truth,* used three times in the introduction. Then follows an admonition to walk in truth, an appeal for a life of love and obedience. John warns against those who pervert the truth by preaching a different doctrine about Christ. Such persons are to be avoided. The letter closes with John's plans to visit this family.

Third John

Third John is addressed to Gaius, an elder in the church. John praises him for walking in the truth and gives instructions about the hospitality to be shown to traveling ministers. Anyone who receives such persons into his house becomes a "fellow-worker for the truth." By way of contrast John reports that a certain Diotrephes needs rebuke because of his ambition and arrogance. A man named Demetrius receives words of praise from the apostle. The letter closes with visitation plans and greetings.

Jude

The letter of Jude, written by the brother of James, bears a strong resemblance to 2 Peter. The book gives a defense of the faith because of deceivers who are trying to undermine it.

Jude describes those people who are rebelling against God's truth. He cites historical examples of divine judgment and compares the deceivers with past figures, depicting their depravity. Admonishing the believers to lead a positive Christian life, he closes with a doxology.

Revelation

The book of Revelation is a revelation of Jesus Christ. Unique in the New Testament, it is addressed to seven churches in Asia Minor and is written against the background of their conflicts with the Roman empire. Against such problems the book gives a message of hope for a glorious future. John wrote the book while suffering persecution as a prisoner on the island of Patmos. He was given a vision of Christ as judge, who commanded him to write in a book "the things which you have seen."

John also describes "the things which are," that is, the present circumstances, and "the things which shall take place after these things."

Interpretation

There are several ways to interpret the final and longest part of the book (4-22), which deals with future events. Some persons apply these chapters to the history of Christianity on earth, including such events as the fall of Rome. Another view sees chapters 2 and 3, the seven letters, as seven time periods of church history before the rapture—when Christ will come again to take away His church—and chapters 4-19 as a description of the events to take place up to the time of Christ's return. These events include the millennium, Christ's thousand-year reign on earth.

What Shall Be

In the introductory vision (4-5), the Lamb that was slain (Christ) is given a scroll with seven seals. With the opening of each seal, new judgments are unleashed on parts of the earth. But 144,000 from Israel, along with a great multitude from all peoples, are spared the judgments (6-7). The seventh seal launches seven judgments, each of which is announced by a trumpet. The last three of these judgments are called "woes." The last "woe" (the last trumpet) signals the return of Christ and the beginning of His glorious kingdom (8-11).

"And I saw a new heaven and a new earth; for the first heaven and the first earth passed away, and there is no longer any sea...And the city has no need of the sun or of the moon to shine upon it, for the glory of God has illumined it, and its lamp is the Lamb" (Revelation 21:1 and 23).

The remainder of the book deals with certain aspects of this period in more detail, in particular the "two signs." The first sign depicts three anti-Christian "beasts," which represent powers: the dragon, the beast from the sea and the beast out of the earth. Connected with all this are seven scenes drawn from the period of the "Great Tribulation" (12-14). The second sign depicts seven new judgments (seven bowls), which are poured out over the earth (15-16). An expanded sequence follows regarding the "great harlot" or "Babylon the Great" (17-18). From there, the book proceeds directly to the return of Christ and the establishment of His kingdom, followed by the last judgment and the creation of a new heaven and a new earth (15-21). A separate vision describes the glorified state of the church, the new Jerusalem, after Christ's return.

The epilogue contains specific exhortations and expresses longing for the Bridegroom; it also includes the promises of Christ and gives a closing benediction (22).

Notes

Chapter 1

1. Rene Pache, *Inspiration & Authority*. Chicago: Moody Press, 1970, pp. 116-117.
2. Josh McDowell and Don Stewart, *Answers to Tough Questions*. San Bernardino, CA: Here's Life Publishers, 1980, pp. 2, 3.
3. Nelson Glueck, *Rivers in the Desert: History of Negev*. Philadelphia, PA: Jewish Publication Society of America, 1969, p. 84.
4. Sidney Collett, *All About the Bible*. Old Tappan, NJ: Fleming H. Revell Publishing Company, n.d., p. 63.
5. Quoted by John Lea, *The Greatest Book in the World*. Philadelphia, PA: n.p., 1922, pp. 17, 18.
6. Isaiah 40:6-8.
7. Charles Woodruff Shields, *The Scientific Evidences of Revealed Religion*. New York: Charles Scribner's Sons, Inc., 1900, p. 27.
8. John B. Noss, *Man's Religions*. New York: The Macmillan Company, 1969, pp. 50, 51.
9. James Orr, s.v. "World: Cosmological," *The International Standard Bible Encyclopaedia*, Vol. 5. Grand Rapids, MI: William B. Eerdmans Publishing Company, 1939, 1956, p. 3107.
10. Frederick A. Filby, *The Flood Reconsidered*. Grand Rapids, MI: Zondervan Publishing House, 1971, p. 93.
11. Wilbur Smith, *Have You Considered Him?* Downers Grove, IL: Inter-Varsity Press, 1970, pp. 8, 9.
12. Isaiah 46:9, 10.
13. Isaiah 48:3-5.
14. For more in-depth treatment of this subject, we recommend Josh McDowell's *Evidence That Demands a Verdict,* published by Here's Life Publishers, San Bernardino, California, ©1972, chapters 9 and 11.
15. Luke 24:25-27.
16. John 5:39, 40.
17. John 1:1, 14, 29.
18. Matthew 24:27, 30, 31.
19. McDowell and Stewart, *Answers,* dedication.
20. E. M. Blaiklock, ed., *Why I Am Still a Christian*. Grand Rapids, MI: Zondervan Publishing House, 1971, p. 16.
21. Deuteronomy 6:4, 5.
22. Isaiah 43:10, 11.
23. 1 Corinthians 8:4-6.
24. Luke 11:9-13.
25. Matthew 5:6.
26. Matthew 11:28-30.
27. John 4:14.
28. John 5:39.
29. John 10:10.
30. Bernard Ramm, *Protestant Christian Evidences*. Chicago, IL: Moody Press, 1953, p. 208.
31. J. M. Houston in *Why I Am Still a Christian,* p. 83.
32. E. Y. Mullins, *Why Is Christianity True?* Chicago, IL: Christian Culture Press, 1905, pp. 284, 285.
33. J. T. Fisher and L. S. Hawley, *A Few Buttons Missing*. Philadelphia: Lippincott, 1951, p. 273.
34. Sir Walter Scott, *The Monastery*. Boston, MA: Houghton Mifflin Company, 1813, p. 140.

Chapter 2

1. Deuteronomy 31:26.
2. Deuteronomy 17:18, 19.

3. H. Danby, trans., *The Mishnah.* London: Oxford University Press, 1967, p. 446.

4. F. F. Bruce, *The Books and the Parchments.* Westwood, NJ: Fleming H. Revell Company, 1963, p. 98.

5. Sir Frederic G. Kenyon, *Our Bible and the Ancient Manuscripts.* New York: Harper and Row, Publishers, 1941, p. 38.

6. Samuel Davidson, *The Hebrew Text of the Old Testament* (2nd ed.) London: Samuel Bagster & Sons, 1859, p. 89.

7. Flavius Josephus, "Flavius Josephus Against Apion," in *Josephus' Complete Works.* William Whiston, trans., Grand Rapids, MI: Kregel Publications, 1960, pp. 179, 180.

8. H. B. Swete, *An Introduction to the Old Testament in Greek.* R. R. Ottley, revisor, New York: KTAV Publishing House, 1902, 1968, pp. 315, 316.

9. Norman L. Geisler and William Nix, *A General Introduction to the Bible.* Chicago: Moody Press, 1968, p. 263.

10. Gleason L. Archer, *A Survey of Old Testament Introduction.* Chicago: Moody Press, 1964, p. 19.

11. F. F. Bruce, *The Books and the Parchments.* Rev. ed. Westwood: Fleming H. Revell Co., 1963, p. 178.

12. Robert Dick Wilson, *A Scientific Investigation of the Old Testament.* Chicago: Moody Press, 1959, pp. 70, 71, 85.

Chapter 3

1. Bruce Metzger, *The Text of the New Testament.* New York and Oxford: Oxford University Press, 1968, p. 30.

2. J. Harold Greenlee, *Introduction to New Testament Textual Criticism.* Grand Rapids, MI: William B. Eerdmans Publishing Company, 1964, p. 13.

3. Bruce Metzger, *Chapters in the History of New Testament Textual Criticism.* Grand Rapids, Eerdmans, 1963, pp. 144, 145.

4. F. F. Bruce, *The New Testament Documents: Are They Reliable?* 5th revised edition. Downers Grove: Inter-Varsity Press, 1972, pp. 16, 17.

5. Bruce Metzger, *The Text of the New Testament.* New York and Oxford: Oxford University Press, 1968, p. 34.

6. Charles Leach, *Our Bible — How We Got It.* Chicago: Moody Press, 1898, pp. 35, 36.

7. Leo Vaganay, *An Introduction to the Textual Criticism of the New Testament.* Trans. by B. V. Miller, London: Sands and Co., 1937, p. 48.

8. Greenlee, *New Testament Textual Criticism,* p. 33.

9. Kirsopp Lake, *Caesarean Text of the Gospel of Mark.* Harvard Theological Revue, Vol. 21, 1928.

10. Bruce M. Metzger, *A Textual Commentary on the Greek New Testament.* London, New York: United Bible Societies, 1971, p. XV, XVI.

11. Greenlee, *New Testament Textual Criticism,* p. 66.

12. Metzger, *Textual Commentary,* p. XVI.

13. Benjamin B. Warfield, *Introduction to Textual Criticism of the New Testament,* seventh edition. London: Hodder and Stoughton, 1907, p. 14.

14. Samuel Tregelles, *Greek New Testament,* prolegomena.

15. Sir Frederick Kenyon, *Our Bible and the Ancient Manuscripts.* New York: Harper and Row Publishers, 1941, p. 23.

16. Sir Frederick Kenyon, *The Bible and Archaeology.* New York: Harper and Row Publishers, 1940, p. 288.

Chapter 4

1. Flavious Josephus, "Flavius Josephus Against Apion," in *Josephus' Complete Works.* Willian Whiston, trans., Grand Rapids, MI: Kregel Publications, 1960, p. 8.

2. Gleason Archer, *A Survey of Old Testament Introduction.* Revised edition. Chicago: Moody Press, 1974, p. 71.

3. Ibid., p. 609.

4. Luke 24:44.

5. Josh McDowell and Don Stewart, *Answers to Tough Questions.* San Bernardino, CA: Here's Life Publishers, 1980, pp. 36-38.

6. Charles F. Pfeiffer, *The Dead Sea Scrolls & The Bible.* Grand Rapids: Baker Book House, 1969, pp. 111-112.

7. 1 John 1:1-3.

8. Luke 1:1-4.

9. 2 Peter 1:16.

10. 1 Corinthians 15:1-4.

11. F. F. Bruce, *The New Testament Documents: Are They Reliable?* Downers Grove, IL: Inter-Varsity Press, 1960, pp. 45, 46.

12. "An Interview with William F. Albright," *Christianity Today,* January 18, 1963.

13. William F. Albright, *From the Stone Age to Christianity.* Baltimore, MD: Johns Hopkins Press, 1946, p. 29.

14. Norman Geisler and William Nix, *A General Introduction to the Bible.* Chicago, IL: Moody Press, 1968, pp. 200,201.

15. J. I. Packer, *God Has Spoken.* Downers Grove, IL: Inter-Varsity Press, 1979, pp. 120-122.

Chapter 5

1. Herman Ridderbos, *The Authority and Inspiration of Scripture.* H. De Jongste, trans., Grand Rapids, MI: Baker Book House, 1963, p. 8.

2. James I. Packer, *Fundamentalism and the Word of God.* Grand Rapids, MI: William B. Eerdmans Publishing Company, 1958, p. 78ff.

3. 2 Timothy 3:16.

4. 2 Peter 1:20, 21.

5. B. B. Warfield, *The Inspiration and Authority of the Bible.* Nutley, NJ: Presbyterian and Reformed Publishing Company, 1948, p. 173.

6. Norman L. Geisler and William Nix, *A General Introduction to the Bible.* Chicago: Moody Press, 1968, p. 29.

7. Galatians 3:16.

8. John 8:58, 59.

9. Bruce Vawter, *Biblical Inspiration.* Philadelphia: Wesminster Press, 1972.

10. John Warwick Montgomery, ed. *God's Inerrant Word: An International Symposium on the Trustworthiness of Scripture,* Minneapolis, MN: Bethany Fellowship, Inc., 1974, p. 33.

11. W. F. Arndt, *Does the Bible Contradict Itself?* St. Louis, MO: Concordia Publishing House, 1976, pp. 13, 14.

Chapter 6

1. F. F. Bruce, *The New Testament Documents: Are They Reliable?* Downers Grove, IL: Inter-Varsity Press, 1960, p. 8.

2. D. J. Wiseman and Edwin Yamauchi, *Archaeology and the Bible.* Grand Rapids, MI: Zondervan Publishing House, pp. 10-13.

3. John Bright, *The Authority of the Old Testament.* London: SCM Press, 1967, p. 130.

4. R. K. Harrison, B. K. Waltke, Donald Guthrie, and Gorden Fee, *Biblical Criticism: Historical, Literary and Textual.* Grand Rapids, MI: Zondervan Publishing House, 1978, pp. 6, 7.

5. Wiseman and Yamauchi, *Archaeology,* pp. 16, 17.

6. William F. Albright, *The Biblical Period from Abraham to Ezra.* New York: Harper and Row, Publishers, 1960, pp. 1, 2.

7. A. R. Millard, "A New Babylonian 'Genesis' Story," in Tyndale Bulletin 18 (1967): 17, 18.

8. Kenneth Kitchen, *Ancient Orient and Old Testament.* Downers Grove, IL: Inter-Varsity, 1966, p. 89.

9. Paul W. Lapp, *Biblical Archaeology and History.* New York: World Publishing Company, 1969, p. 107.

10. Ibid., p. 111.

11. Harrison, et al., *Biblical Criticism,* pp. 14, 15.

12. Clifford Wilson, *Rocks, Relics and Biblical Reliability.* Grand Rapids, MI: Zondervan, 1977, pp. 88-90.

13. Hermann Schultz, *Old Testament Theology.* H. A. Patterson, trans., Edinburgh: T. & T. Clark, 1848, pp. 25, 26.

14. Wiseman and Yamauchi, *Archaeology,* p. 25.

15. Cyrus Gordon, "Higher Critics and Forbidden Fruit," *Christianity Today,* November 23, 1959.

16. W. F. Albright, "Historical and Mythical Elements in the Story of Joseph," *Journal of Biblical Literature,* vol. 37, 1918.

17. Wiseman and Yamauchi, *Archaeology,* pp. 142, 143.

18. John Elder, *Prophets, Idols, and Diggers.* New York: Bobbs-Merrill Company, 1960, p. 75.
19. Fred H. Wight, *Highlights of Archaeology in Bible Lands.* Chicago: Moody Press, 1955, pp. 94, 95.
20. Bright, *Old Testament,* p. 77.

Chapter 7

1. William F. Albright, "Archaeology," in *The Teacher's Yoke,* E. J. Vardaman, ed. Waco, TX: Baylor University Press, 1964, p. 29.
2. Sir William Ramsey, *St. Paul: The Traveler and Roman Citizen.* Grand Rapids, MI: Baker Book House, 1962, p. 36.
3. Ibid., p. 81.
4. Sir William Ramsey, *The Bearing of Recent Discoveries on the Trustworthiness of the New Testament.* Grand Rapids, MI: Baker Book House, 1953, p. 222.
5. Luke 2:1-5.
6. Gleason L. Archer, Jr., *An Encyclopedia of Bible Difficulties.* Grand Rapids, MI: Zondervan Publishing House, 1981, pp. 365, 366.
7. D. J. Wiseman and Edwin Yamauchi, *Archaeology and the Bible.* Grand Rapids, MI: Zondervan Publishing House, pp. 84-86.
8. E. M. Blaiklock, *The Archaeology of the New Testament.* Grand Rapids, MI: Zondervan, 1970, pp. 79-82.
9. Ibid., pp. 102, 103.
10. F. F. Bruce, *The New Testament Documents: Are They Reliable?* Downers Grove, IL: Inter-Varsity Press, 1960, p. 95.
11. E. M. Blaiklock, *The Archaeology of the New Testament.* Grand Rapids, MI: Zondervan Publishing House, 1974, p. 109.
12. K. A. Kitchen, *The Bible in Its World: The Bible and Archaeology Today.* Downers Grove, IL: Inter-Varsity Press, 1977, pp. 132, 133.
13. Bruce, *Documents,* p. 94.
14. Edwin Yamauchi, *The Stones and the Scriptures.* Philadelphia and New York: J. B. Lippincott Company, 1972, pp. 103, 104.
15. Luke 1:1-4.
16. Luke 3:1, 19; cf. Matthew 14:1, 9. Kitchen, *The Bible,* p. 132.
17. 2 Peter 1:16.
18. Hebrews 1:1-3a.

INDEX

173

ILLUSTRATION CREDITS

The location of the illustrations is indicated by the following abbreviations and combinations thereof:

l. = left   r. = right   t. = top   b. = bottom   c. = center

The editors of this book have made every effort to trace the source of all illustrations. In some cases this was not possible. Claims should be submitted to the Publisher, who agrees to pay any fees due.